I0558179

Nightmares Among Us
13 Stories of Suspense and Terror

Caleb Bundon
Cover Art by Blakely Bundon

Parson's Porch Books

Nightmares Among Us: 13 Stories of Suspense and Terror
ISBN: Softcover 978-1-960326-34-8
Copyright © 2023 by Caleb Bundon

All rights reserved. No part of this book may be reproduced or transmitted in any form or by any means, electronic or mechanical, including photocopying, recording, or by any information storage and retrieval system, without permission in writing from the publisher.

Parson's Porch Books is an imprint of Parson's Porch *&* Company (PP*&*C) in Cleveland, Tennessee. PP*&*C is a self-funded charity which earns money by publishing books of noted authors, representing all genres. Its face and voice is **David Russell Tullock** who you can contact at: dtullock@parsonsporch.com.

Parson's Porch *&* Company *turns books into bread & milk* by sharing its profits with the poor.

www.parsonsporch.com

Nightmares Among Us

Contents

Introduction

Nightmares Among Us is a compilation of several horror stories into one novella or short novel. The first story is about a character in the western ages being trapped by a group of bandits with a secret. A horrifying secret! The second story is about a group of people searching in the sea for abnormal sounds and beings. What they come across is something that they never will forget! The third story is about a person who is surrounded by mysterious disappearances. His friends are disappearing, and he doesn't know where to turn until something mysterious happens to him. The fourth story is about a man who works for a shipping company near a set of train tracks. It just so happens that the train tracks are the source of all the abnormality in this story, and when all the chaos is happening, they would never guess what was truly happening! The fifth story is a horror story about a journal and a 20-dollar bill. These items are not ordinary objects. They will be a crucial part of the main character's future…and his downfall! The sixth story is about a soldier from the oil wars. In this story, his team surrenders, and are then transported to a facility. The facility is full of monsters and creatures that will kill you as soon as you look at them! The seventh story is about a normal human being. As the story advances, he realizes that he is not alone in his house. Thousands of generations of demons haunt his house! The eighth story is about a group of people who are traveling to Mars. They come to realize that there are murderers on the ship, and the only thing that surrounds them is the blankless void of space! The ninth story is about the Titanic. However, the main character encounters multiple strange occurrences! The tenth story is about a boy who goes through something that no boy should. There is a murderer in the city! And when death strikes, what will happen? The eleventh story is a realistic fiction story about me and several others who are locked in a hospital. People who I thought were my friends are now my enemies! The twelfth story is about a seemingly infinite hotel with monsters lurking around every corner, waiting to kill you! And finally, the thirteenth story is about a person who gets lost in the Backrooms, a place of infinitely generated, dull-yellow office complexes and several entities that thirst for blood! You have now heard about all of the stories that this book has to offer. Please, feel free to read this book…and allow yourself to be taken on a journey of a lifetime!

Story I

Lurking

This story takes place in the early 1900s, or in other words, the Western era. The location is a desert. The main character is a single, middle-class man living in the United States. This story is science/historical fiction and involves several elements of surprise and tension. The main character is in his late 20s and is in the prime of his life. His name is John Taylor.

At the defining crow of the rooster, John Taylor rose from his bed. He walked over to the window and opened it. He peered out at the beautiful rising sun and the ever-expanding desert before him. After taking a long look at the scenery, he walked over to his bedside candle and lit it with a match. He went around his cabin, lighting a few oil lamps. Then he got his buffalo rifle; it was hunting time. Since refrigerators did not exist, John couldn't freeze the meat and had to use salt to preserve it. He hunted big game like buffalo, bears, and other animals. No meat meant no breakfast for John. He grabbed an axe off the table, just in case. He stepped outside into the heat and the early rising sun and got on his horse. She was a Tennessee walking horse named Rose. He rode a certain distance away from his house, where he went up a small dune so he could spot the buffalo at a distance. He didn't spot any buffalo, but he did spot a bear.

He needed between 1-3 well-placed headshots to kill a bear. He aimed…he pulled the trigger. **KA-POW!** The shot struck home, a little low, but significantly injured the bear. As the bear charged toward him, he reloaded swiftly, and another shot rang out like crashing thunder on a rare rainy night. The bear collapsed to the ground in a heap. He reloaded his gun just in case. He walked over to the fallen bear and began skinning it. He took the bear's hide and meat and carried it a short distance away to his horse, Rose. John strapped the hide and meat to her and then rode back to his cabin.

He jumped off the horse with a force strong as a bull but quiet as the notorious Jim Miller.[1] John walked over to the door of his cabin. It was almost time for his job to start. When he opened the door, John walked over to the furnace, lit it using wood, oil, and matches, and began cooking the meat. He had to be very careful about how much meat he ate; the price of meat had gone up, and he would sell the meat he didn't eat. He chopped off a small ½ lb. slice of meat which contained little fat and tossed it into the furnace. It was pretty warm and about as hot as a grill by now. Once

---

[1] Miller was a famous outlaw born in 1861 and nicknamed "Deacon Jim" for attending a Methodist church. He was one of the worst outlaws of the western era!

the meat was cooked, he carefully pulled it out with some tongs and diced the meat into cubes. John then sprinkled a special seasoning on the diced bear and sat down to eat.

Not even ten minutes later, John rose from his chair and extinguished the oil lamps. He saddled up his horse and rode into town. Oddly enough, Rose seemed slower and out of breath, but he decided to continue into town. Inside the town, he first spotted the general store. To the left was the guns and weapons shop, and to the right was the saloon where he worked. He liked being an entertainer there, and a few weeks ago, he was officially hired, making about $.75 an hour. It might not sound like much, but that equates to approximately $25 an hour today!

As he walked in, he heard the deafening sound of people shouting, chatting, singing and eating breakfast. John wentstraight to the piano and started playing. On the first note, everyone got silent. He started playing the new popular piece "The Maple Leaf Rag" by Scott Joplin. He listened to all the notes as he played, making sure they synchronized. When he finished playing, the place erupted in a storm of cheers! John continued to play the piano throughout the day. Around sunset, people began to leave. His boss, Will Moore, dismissed him early. By the time he was home, he was quite tired. He didn't stay up long; he quickly extinguished the oil lamps and went to sleep.

John Taylor woke up the following day feeling refreshed and awake. Today, all the townspeople were excused from their jobs. Today was the day of the auction! Most of the town will attend, and the train will depart the station at 8:00 AM. John got up and noticed his timepiece was missing. He thought, "No matter! Hopefully, it's not yet 8:00 AM!" He grabbed two quarters and a sack of money and headed out to town. A train ran through several neighboring towns, including where the auction was held, which was several miles away in the mountains. Once he arrived in town, he paid $.25 to the person managing the train tickets, equating to about $8.00 today. John was told that the 8:00 AM train would arrive at the station in ten minutes. He ran to the saloon, bought a meal and drink for $.25, and then sprinted back like the wind on an April day. About five minutes later, it arrived, and John boarded the train.

It was crowded on the train, but he managed to squeeze his way into a seat. A minute or two later, the train started rolling. Not much happened on the train; there was some chatter, but that was it. Ten minutes later, the train screeched to an abrupt halt at the station. Everyone got off the train and walked around to the auction center. The auction center is called "Will's Auction Center," but everyone calls it the auction house. A legend goes around that they make over $75 a day! That totals over $4,000 a year![2] John believed the legend because people spent all their money at the auction, and the auction was held 2 to 4 times a month! Five minutes later the auction began. The first item on auction was a Mauser 1893. Its starting price was $76.[3] The next item on sale was a German Mauser Pistol with a starting price of $61.[4] The following product was a premium souped-up LeMat revolver for a starting price of $30.[5] The final item was a new Harmonica Gun. Its starting price was $32.[6] The Mauser 1893 sold swiftly. Only 10 minutes passed before someone bought it for $92.[7] After the Mauser 1893 was sold, the next product sold was the German Mauser Pistol. It sold for an insane $123![8] It took 20 minutes for it to sell. The Lemat Revolver took a long 30 minutes to sell. It sold for $60.[9]

The final product, the Harmonica Gun, was the one that took the shortest to sell. Nobody wanted it, so John got it for a mere $40![10] After the final bid, everybody headed outside to the train. There was an enormous clock on the front of the auction building,

---

[2]$2,500 and $135,000
[3]$2,500
[4]$2,100
[5]$1,000
[6]$1,100
[7]$3,150
[8]$4,325
[9]$2,000
[10]$1,350

and it read that the time was 9:15 AM. Once everyone was on the train, it started moving. John was amazed that he had won the Harmonica Gun! At this very moment, the sound of gunfire reached his ears, yet the train continued as if nothing had happened. The people, however, started ducking as John heard a distinct sound. The sound is known today as a siren, but at this time and in this era, it was almost supernatural! Sirens did not even exist until the 20th century!

As people ducked and bullets rained down, John aimed his Harmonica Gun at the now broken window. Clink! The gun was not loaded! He quickly loaded the gun and aimed for a bandit. He spotted one outside of the train, only ten yards away, riding on his horse. **KA-POW!** He fired a shot. The horse stumbled but kept galloping. The bandit saw John and fired three shots. All of them missed because John ducked and hid behind a door. John looked again and noticed that the bandit had boarded the train and was coming through the entrance to his train car. John hid, and when the bandit came through, John fired two shots which ended the bandit's life. When John walked through the door between the passenger compartment and the engine, he was hit with a blunt object and was knocked out…

When he regained consciousness, he was in a cool, dimly lit place. There was a man in the room, and he said, "Ahh, John! You're awake. Good." To which

John replied, "Who are you?! Where am I?! What…is this place?" The man replied, "First answer, I am Jim Miller. I know that you've heard of me. I am a thirty-three-year-old bandit known as the worst of the west." John pleads, "Why me, though? Why did you kidnap me?" Jim Miller replied, "You killed one of our bandits. As for where you are, you are in our camp…well, actually, you are underneath the camp. You are in the mines. Your Harmonica Gun will make a fine addition to my collection!" John fearfully replied, "What will happen to me?!" Jim Miller said, "Oh, we aren't going to kill you! No…no, that would be wasteful! We're going to make you work in this very mine! And if you escape, we will release our secret…uh…weapon on you, if you consider it a weapon. It is a tree-like figure as tall as a pine tree! It also has a siren for the head. The siren sounds like an eerie Harpsichord. We call the creature The Ignotum!" A bandit behind him then blindfolded John, and the bandit escorted him to the mines.

John was in the mine, mining for days with little water or food until Jim Miller came to see him one day. "Hello. Are you enjoying the torture of mining?" He did not give John enough time to answer. "We are leaving to make a little raid on the bank in your town! We will leave you here, but if you try to escape…you will perish!" Jim Miller then walked away without saying a word. Surprisingly, no bandits had been left there to ensure that John wouldn't escape!

John noticed that the rope used to bind his hands to the ground and wall was pretty loose, so he started moving his wrists to create friction. After doing this for what seemed like an eternity, he managed to free himself from the grasp of the rope. When he exited the mine, John immediately noticed it was nightfall. A sundial told him that it was 9:30 in the evening. He caught sight of his Harmonica Gun leaning against a wall. They didn't even take it with them! John took the gun and made his way out of the camp. He was free! John also saw some horses nearby, so he jumped on one and headed towards the nearest town.

The ride to town took only a few minutes. He took a train back to his hometown and got off the train when it stopped at the mill. Just outside the mill, there was a mine and a forest. He walked to a nearby chest and got an axe. He did not believe this "secret weapon" Jim Miller had told him about really existed. He did not notice the siren sound until the leaves and trees started rustling! John froze. He looked around, grabbed his Harmonica Gun, and advanced toward the sound of the leaves and "siren." He nearly ran into a rotting tree. The tree had enormous roots and smelled very odd. He shot it out of curiosity, and the tree started moving! This was no rotting tree! It was The Ignotum!
As he opened fire, the enormous being became enraged and picked John up! The siren sound was deafening because it was right in front of him! John,

paralyzed with fear, couldn't even scream. The Ignotum then tossed him into his siren, which doubled as a mouth! Before succumbing to the darkness, John prayed that his death would be quick…

Story II

Point Nemo

This story is based on past events and is a combination of historical fiction and science fiction. An ordinary person with a history of sea-related adventures has another adventure awaiting him! Despite all of this, he couldn't prepare for what would happen! The date is November 1997 and takes place in Atlanta, Georgia and New Orleans. This is the story of Kevin Rogers.

Hello, my name is Kevin Rogers. I am 39 years old, and I was born on January 31 in New Orleans. I was born into a Christian family and was baptized when I was 12 on October 27, 1970. We had a simple two-story house with modern amenities. Several years later, I attended college in New Orleans for Marine life and business. After finishing school, I went home and worked two part-time jobs. One was at McDonald's and the other was working at an institution with sea life. The workers there were pleasant and helpful. Nothing much happened when I first started working. That was until 1997, when I was riding home in my Toyota Camry. After parking, I went inside.

I was about to go to bed when the doorbell rang. I walked over to the door and opened it. Outside stood a man in his late 30s. I said "Hello? What purpose brings you to my door?" He then said, "Hello. My name is Mr. Thompson. I am from a secret organization whose job is to capture strange anomalies from different areas of the world. My site is SCP area 404. I have come to ask you to register for the Atlantic Anomalies Search." I responded with, "Ok. What is it, and where might it be located?" Mr. Thompson replied, "Atlanta, GA. As for when it is, whenever you please. If you choose to join, you will be the final squad member, and bring our total to 6. I came to you because you seem to have enough skill to execute what is ordered." I replied, "Very well. I will notify my job operator that I have been asked to move to a new job." Mr. Thompson said, "That is a good plan. I need you to sign a few pages of paperwork." I welcomed Mr. Thompson inside and filled out the paperwork. After bidding Mr. Thompson farewell, I started planning a train route to Atlanta that would leave at 9:15 AM the following day.

The next morning, I drove 4 miles to the New Orleans train station and boarded the train. I paid $50 for a coach seat. The train arrived in Atlanta, GA at midnight. When I got there, several people greeted me. The entire group loaded up on a bus, which took us to the coast, where we boarded a large boat. It was very spacious with several amenities including queen beds in every room, a jacuzzi, a good-sized dining table with room for 12, several of the newest phones in every room, and many other amenities. Everyone carried a weapon since they were going to a spot in the ocean *thousands* of miles away! The Mariana Trench! The first few days were fairly uneventful. On day one, as we passed Cuba and Florida, we felt a disturbance in the ship.

Somehow, the generator was slightly waterlogged. Luckily, it only took a day to fix. On day 3, the ship and the entire crew went through customs as we entered the Panama Canal. We had to dock for two days. After that, we had an enormous expanse of sea to cover. A few hours later, we all heard something. It was a low-frequency sound, almost like a hum, but more sinister! Several watertight compartments malfunctioned, and we had electricity problems for a few hours. Everyone prayed that we would reach the nearest island in time!

Thankfully we reached the island! We found an unknown material that was hot to the touch, which turned out to be a mix of several different metals and gasses. All of these materials turned out to be radioactive! It cost us upwards of $10,000 to fix! After going through customs *again*, we moved to our seventh day at sea. The boat was now experiencing even *more* problems; this time, it was the rudder chain. We had 4 days and 16 hours until we reached Hawaii, so we needed to work fast! I had taken some types of engineering classes in college, so I was able to fix it in a short amount of time before it got out of hand. The only problem was that we had to stop the boat for a good 16 hours. After that, we were finally on our way.

The next night, I heard something sinister. I had a busy night, which included going to the jacuzzi and playing Sega's USA Daytona Beach. I finally went to sleep, but 3 hours later I was awoken by a noise! It is hard to explain it almost sounded like a train or something going past our ship! I peeked out the small window and saw an eerie white sea creature retreating into the water. I couldn't move! I was shivering with terror! I looked and saw that the bottom of the ship was filling with water. We still had several thousand miles to go to Hawaii! I woke everyone I could find, and we helped to fix the boat. No one believed me about the sea creature, and it took the entirety of the trip to Hawaii to fix the problems with the ship. Thankfully, one person had the bright idea to go search on the radar and spectrogram sound detector. Davis quickly found the files on a special floppy disc, but we couldn't read it until we reached Hawaii.

Nothing much happened until after we arrived…

When we arrived in Hawaii, we had been on the boat for 12 days. It had felt more like 6, however. While there, Davis picked up a second noise, and we were able to play it back. The noise was very similar to what

I had heard earlier in the trip. They predicted that it was the high-pitched wail of an iceberg. However, the nearest iceberg cluster was about 2,300 miles away! Strangely enough, they still believed that an iceberg struck the ship. The gash on the ship looked like that was what indeed had happened. The cost to repair the ship this time was a fee of $15,000! As we analyzed the second sound file, it revealed a "boing" sound with interesting waves in the spectrogram.

The crew asked if I had heard that sound before. I thought hard: I heard the sound when I was playing Sega late at night, but I thought it was a game sound. This time, everyone believed me. A local in Hawaii then said, "You say that it was a "boing" sound?" Everyone said yes in unison. The local said, "Ahh, yes. There is a sea creature that roams Hawaii. It emits a 'boing-like' sound and has done so since 1976!" Davis and I said, "Interesting!" The local said something that immediately sparked our attention and got our adrenaline running! "The sea creature has recently been spotted! It was first spotted only a year ago!" Everyone started asking different questions. I asked, "How vast is it?" The local described it as slightly smaller than a submarine.

After staying a night in Hawaii, we headed to the Northern Mariana Islands. The Northern Mariana Islands were a group of islands near the Mariana Trench. The captain made a *big* mistake after we left

Hawaii! He strayed off course, and badly! Instead of going to the Northern Mariana Islands, the captain went too far north, and we ended up in Alaska! While there, we discovered that there were some interesting formations of icebergs. We gathered the equipment to go on the ice, weapons, in case we encountered an animal, and scuba gear. We all gathered on the ship's deck and the captain dismissed all of us, except for Davis. He was staying behind voluntarily to search for the water's sound waves. Now *that's* dedication!

We jumped in the water, which didn't feel that cold since our wetsuits had a heater pack installed. Anyways, we swam around in the ocean for a little bit. We saw lots of sea life there! God's nature is beautiful! I heard something in the water; it was the sound of a humpback whale hunting. The humpback whale isn't a sinister sea creature, but the sound was still very eerie. It stopped suddenly, and I then heard a low roaring sound. It sounded similar to that of an engine, but our ship engines did not sound exactly like that. I decided to go to the source of the noise. There was a droning sound like something sliding down. After some searching, I finally saw it: the sound was an iceberg collapsing into the ocean.

Since I was so focused on the iceberg, I did not seem to notice a sea creature approaching me. It startled me at first when I finally noticed it, but I then realized that it was just a beluga whale. I was shocked by the fact that it started "speaking" what sounded similar to human words! However, I couldn't make out any of the words uttered by the animal. I climbed on the ice where the rest of the team was gathered. The captain's name was Smith. Smith said, "Crew and fellow friends, do you wish to plow through the ice? Or do you wish to head back to the ship?" All but one crew member wished to go back to the ship. At that very moment, Davis shouted from a megaphone, "Guys! I think I've got something!" We jumped into the water and swam back to the ship.

After we were safely on board, we all changed and took showers while Davis recovered the sound files. While we were on the ice, Davis said he saw a weird-looking sea creature, almost like a dolphin. Davis also recorded strange sound files. They were very faint; he said it could have come from 10,000 miles away! We then headed toward The Northern Mariana Islands. The journey would take a little over 4 days. We are currently on day 18 of our trip. Finally, Davis found the sound files! The first few were the sounds I heard, but then there was a sound that no one had heard. This sound was almost like a weird pinging sound; it was indescribable. Yes, it could be machinery, but all signs indicate it is not a machine. There were no ships in the area. We continued along our journey. On day 22, we were just under 300 miles away from Guam, the largest island in the chain of The North Mariana Islands, when we heard a whale. But the sound Davis picked up was very eerie. It sounded…somewhat lonely.

When we docked in Guam, we went through customs and stayed a night in a hotel. After a restful night at the hotel, we all got back on the boat and made our way to the Mariana Trench. I could tell everyone was nervous; however, I was not. Davis decided to turn on the news, and we saw that a weird dolphin had swum ashore! I say weird because it was blind and had razor-sharp teeth! The craziest thing was that it came ashore in Alaska! An hour later, we were right over the trench's deepest point. Davis dropped a Remotely Operated Vehicle in the water with special equipment, and for 20 minutes, there was just the sound of sloshing of water.

That was until Davis heard a strange sound. It was almost like a whale, but sinister! It also wavered. The ROV continued to plummet downward for a few more minutes before we heard another unknown sound. After that, the ROV stopped recording. No one spoke; we were in utter shock at what happened. We did not notice anything around us. What arose from the water was an enormous sea creature. It was so large that it would dwarf any ship at that time. The first person to notice it was Davis. It was his scream of terror that awoke us from our shocked trance. After that, the boat swayed a good 5 meters, and everyone went flying!

The sea creature had damaged the stern and had disabled the engine. All of the lifeboats were knocked into the dark water below and sank. One person fell through a glass window on the ship and broke his neck! It killed him instantly! He fell into the water and sank 6 miles before the pressure of the water evaporated his already broken body! Another person was flung into the glass and knocked unconscious. The captain nearly had the same fate as the two others had he not caught himself just in time. I was jolted forward into the transmitter tower. Everyone else was just tossed around. The boat corrected itself, however, it could not stop the bleeding of the water. I looked up, and saw that Smith was headed to the deathly black water. I was able to save him just in time. When I had made sure he was not severely injured, the sea creature had disappeared. We only had 5 others left. Smith ran down below the decks and announced that the boat was collecting water and would inevitably sink.

The captain then saw that all the lifeboats were gone. He said that our best hope was to get a life vest on. I shouted, "What about him?!" I pointed to where the one unnamed person was. Smith responded solemnly, "He must be left behind." Davis then shouted, "I need to transmit one final message!" Davis ran over to the transmitter tower and started punching in morse code. Smith, me, and the two other crew members jumped into the water below. It was colder than I had expected. Much colder! Deathly cold. It was at this moment that we knew we had made a fatal mistake. We did not get on our scuba gear! Also, at that unfortunate time, the transmitter tower collapsed. Davis was able to dodge it, but while trying to dodge it, he slipped and fell, and the tower pinned him down. A series of electric sparks followed suit. The sparks did not dissipate. They continued down the pole and made contact with Davis. There was another person left on the ship. **KA-BOOM!** The ship exploded in a rain of sparks and fire. There were now only 3 people left. Smith said that we were over 200 miles from land. Our bodies were starting to go numb with cold. An hour passed, and once that happened, we could not hold on any longer. We had to succumb to the darkness…

Davis' Last Message:

... --- ... / ... .--. / .... .. -. -.- .. -. --. / -- .- .-. .. .- -. .-
/ - .-. . -. -.-. .... / .---- ----. ----. --... / --- -.-. - --- -... . .-.
/ .---- ...-- / .... . .- / -.-. .-. .. .- - .. - -. . -. . .

Story III

Chaos

This realistic fictional story takes place in April of 2007 in Orlando, Florida. The main character, Robert Young, is an average young man. He is 15 years old, and he is a Christian.

Ding! The school bell rang shrilly to signal the end of school. Robert was happy to get out of class and drive home. He saw people getting into expensive cars and revving their engines at other students. A smirk crossed Robert's face. "One day, they will destroy the bumper or some other car part while in their expensive cars. And instead of paying $100 for repairs, they will spend well over $1,000!" He walked over to his car, which was a white Toyota truck, and opened the door. He put his bag in the passenger seat and started the car. It took about 5 minutes to get home, where he said hello to his mom Hannah and went upstairs to work on homework. Reviewing Math One was not too difficult. He laughed at all of the good memories of that class. All of his friends had helped him throughout the course. He finished his homework around 4:00 PM and then played his favorite PS2 game, Star Wars Battlefront II. He loved everything that involved destroying evil. After playing for a bit, he ate dinner, bid his mom farewell to her night shift job, and turned on the TV.

The football game he was watching was interrupted by an amber alert. The news anchor announced that two teenagers had vanished without a trace! Robert did not think much of it until the TV called out the name of his friend, Lucas. Robert's heart stopped at the news. His crush's name was Ava, and Lucas was her best friend. Robert sprinted to his room to grab his phone off his bedside table, but it wasn't there. He quickly glanced around the room and spotted his phone on his dresser. He grabbed it and punched in Ava's number, but she did not respond. He left her a message; "Hello, it's Robert. I was watching TV when an amber alert came on for your friend Lucas. I am so sorry! I can't imagine what you must be going through right now! Let me know if there is anything that I can help you with." He ended the call and put down the phone. He ran his fingers through his hair. He already had a stressful week with school, and now this! He took a few deep breaths. Robert returned to the TV, which was now broadcasting the weather as light rain and a long sunset. He looked out the window at the approaching cumulonimbus clouds. "It looks like you are accurate for once!" Robert said to the TV.

He got up and walked over to the door. He got his raincoat from the hook by the door and zipped it up before going for a walk. He also grabbed pepper spray, just in case. After walking for about 15 minutes, it started to rain, and the little droplets quickly increased into sheets of rain. By this time, he had reached the Amtrak station, which was about 20 minutes away from his house. It was very foggy! He took a look around, and he discovered that the Amtrak station was eerily deserted. It was almost as if the place was abandoned. Suddenly, Robert spotted someone in the shadows. Carefully, Robert started walking toward them, and the stranger turned at the sound of footsteps.

Robert caught just a glimpse of the stranger's face. "Hello there," Robert said. "Funny how this Amtrak station is so deserted; it's unnatural, even unsettling!" At that moment, the stranger and Robert made eye contact. "Lucas?!" Robert shouted, startling the crows in the trees near the station. Next, he ran over to put his hands on Lucas's shoulders, but when he did that, Robert seemingly melted through Lucas and fell on the rocks at the feet of the track! He rolled over to see Lucas staring at him solemnly. Lucas said, "Watch out for him. He craves flesh and blood!" Lucas then faded into the dense, misty fog around Robert.

Robert lay there for a minute, just beside the track, when he heard a train blow its horn. Robert moved just in time. Swoosh! The train roared past him! If he had moved a second later, he would be dead! After that, he thought to himself, "What was that?! Was I hallucinating? Or was it something else?" Robert sprinted home. When he got home, he was soaking wet and very shaken. He sank to his knees and asked himself... "Am I going insane?!" His stomach started churning. He yelled, "**NO!**" He took a few deep breaths, and whispered to himself, "Breathe, in and out, inhale and exhale." He checked his phone and discovered that Ava had responded to his call with a message back. "Hi, Robert. Thank you for calling me! I needed someone to remind me that I still had at least one other friend. The police finished questioning me and just sent out a search party. Can I please come over to your house tomorrow? I would like to talk to you." Robert replied, "Yes, as long as my parents say it's okay." After this, he got ready for bed, and went to sleep. He had nightmares about Lucas that night. It had been a long and trying day for Robert.

The next day, the school was out due to all the accumulated rain. Robert told his parents about last night's escapade; they thought he had hallucinated. Robert did not press the matter because he did not feel the urgency. For all he knew, he could have hallucinated and not even seen Lucas! His parents did allow Ava to come over to their house mainly because Ava knew Robert well. Robert's parents left the teens at home to help with the search for Lucas. Robert's parents left at 10:00 AM, just as Ava and her family arrived. After Robert's family left, Robert and Ava sat at the table talking about Lucas's disappearance. Ava recalled her last conversation with Lucas regarding prayer requests he had. Lucas's only prayer request dealt with school struggles. After they ended the call, Lucas disappeared a mere one and one-half hours later; he had vanished without a trace!

The police were baffled but still consented to search the vicinity. Robert brought up the previous night's peculiar adventure while talking to Ava. When he got to the part about Lucas, Ava asked, "Are you one hundred percent certain it was Lucas? Would you say it was Lucas if it was on your life?" Robert responded, "Yes to both." When Robert finished the story, Ava said she could picture one of two scenarios that happened that night. One scenario was that Lucas had come back as an angel of some sort to warn Robert about the person who kidnapped him, or possibly that Robert imagined things. Both were possibilities. After their conversation, nothing much happened. Ava informed the police of what had happened to Robert, and the police questioned him. He got the same reaction as Ava had: confusion. Nobody could explain it any differently. After Robert met with the police, he joined the search party and searched until nightfall. Once home, Robert turned on the TV before going to bed. He noticed that the sunset was shorter tonight, which was interesting! Robert fell asleep on the couch.

The next day Robert went to church. Robert's church family seemed discouraged since the police had not found anything. At church, everyone prayed over Lucas' family before leaving. Robert had a different idea; rather than helping the search group today, he got on his computer and looked up everything he could about Lucas. His story had been uploaded to the missing person page. He kept searching, but nothing turned up. He decided to explore the dark web. He did not find the dark web; instead, he found a page on the internet where all the mysteries of the internet were located. The deep web. He only found one page devoted to a discussion page and missing person cases in Orlando, FL. Oddly enough, the page and discussion were up even though Lucas' case had been out briefly. With it came several links. Robert double-checked if the VPN was working on his computer. It was. He then opened the discussion page. One post said, "I am worried about the crime rate in Orlando. Crime has been on the rise for some time, and now it's at a peak we have not seen for over half of a century!" Some other discussions were fairly uninteresting.

However, there was one discussion post that changed the tide of everything! Someone released a png file containing an email sent from the user "Anno Advolvit." The description was in Latin but translated to, "I am watching you, Lucas. You will be the first to die. You have three days. Good luck outrunning your grave." When Robert saw this, he checked the date. It was sent at midnight, just three hours before the amber alert came on his tv after Lucas went missing. Robert looked at the date and time. He had only 15 hours left, according to the post!

At that very moment, the page refreshed, this time by a user named Cain S. It was a picture of a house, and the house was very unsettling! It looked abandoned, like something out of a horror film! However, the caption was the most chilling part. The caption stated only binary code that translated to this. "Bodies decompose three times faster in water than they do on land. I will put this into use in 15 hours." Robert's heart nearly stopped. He reached for his phone and took a picture of the page. Once he lowered his camera, the page crashed. It was an error 401. An error 401 is an HTTP error when the servers can't open the page due to the URL being unauthenticated. Robert restarted the computer to find that the page had a 404 error, meaning the file, or link in this case, was absent…non-existent. Robert shut down the computer and ran to the search party.

Robert told the police, and the police summoned Lucas's and Ava's family. They were stunned! Ava said, "I have heard of someone named Cain S! I don't know his last name. Otherwise, he would have been located by now. Cain was, and still is, an urban legend in Florida. He is a serial killer who killed at least 4 people from 1990 to today!" The police expanded their search to the lakes and coast of Florida. They continued looking for 15 hours and found nothing. Robert decided to boot up his computer again. He tried returning to the website, and this time, it let Robert in. Robert discovered another post from Cain. This time, the caption was labeled "Contents - Unknown." The png attached to the document was a picture of the water with a murky brown spot straight ahead of the camera.

They sent the information to the police and the entire search party. Thankfully, the page never had any errors and was running suspiciously smoothly. Three hours later, there was another post, this time showing a lake. The search party extended to all over Florida rather than mainly the coastline. Robert only had to wait until noon when another post appeared. This time, it showed a road. No one could decide where it was. Then the final post appeared at midnight. This time, a picture of Lake Lucerne. Robert notified the police to search the lake. They found the body of Lucas with hundreds of puncture wounds from what appeared to be nails! Everyone was stunned! The S.W.A.T. team went to every house nearby and thoroughly searched for them, but nothing was found. The search for Lucas was closed, and Cain was never located.

Lucas's family members were deeply saddened. School was canceled on Monday because of the funeral for Lucas. After the funeral, Cain was placed on the most wanted list. The next day, Robert went to Ava's house and discussed the events from the last few days. Robert brought over his dad's laptop and went to the same link where he found all the posts. The username had been updated to read Cain Schizophrenia. The last name was fascinating, since Schizophrenia is a mental disorder where the person reacts to life abnormally. Robert informed the S.W.A.T. team, and they updated their findings. After comforting Ava, Robert went home to relax and unwind. While watching TV, the news said that the sunset was said to be the shortest it has been in over a decade! Robert fell asleep watching the sunset.

The following school week went by in almost a trance-like state. The school's most popular student was now Ava. On Saturday, Robert invited Ava over to his house again, but Ava couldn't come because she had something to do. She said, "Maybe tomorrow after church." Robert agreed, and after going to church on Sunday, he called Ava, but she did not answer. Robert left a message. "Hey, it's Robert. You said after church today you could come over to my house. I just wanted to check if you were coming." Robert gulped. He was contemplating whether he should tell Ava that he had a crush on her. "I know you must be going through a lot right now, but I can't keep this a secret anymore. I have a crush on you! You are just the best friend that I could hope for! I think that is all for now. Goodbye!" Robert set down the phone. "Whew!" Robert exclaimed. "That got a lot off of my chest!" Robert sat down on the couch and turned on the TV.

That emotion he was feeling was short-lived. When he turned on the TV, it switched to an Amber alert for none other than Ava! His heart stopped for one beat; he couldn't bear it. Not Ava! The call proclaiming his feelings for Ava…it was meaningless! That is…unless he found Ava. He opened his computer and went back to the website. Sure enough, the mysterious Cain had Ava. The caption read, "If you are not careful, Ava will be second! If you are careful, you will be second!" For the second time that night, Robert's heart seemed to stop. Robert looked at the comments that he had not noticed before. There was only one comment. It read, "I am watching you, Robert." Robert got his phone and his pepper spray, and went to the family safe, which contained many of their guns and valuables. Robert unlocked the safe and promised to only neutralize someone if he had to. Robert took his dad's Spas-12 shotgun and 24 rounds of ammo. He also took his dad's Desert Eagle and 24 rounds of ammo. He took the armored vest and suited up. Before closing the safe, he took the S.W.A.T. grade baton to defend himself. Robert also managed to take a knife and flashlight. He closed the safe and headed out in his car to Lake Lucerne.

He drove 2 minutes to the lake. He was very cautious. Robert walked around the houses until he found the house in the picture from one of the posts. He looked at the door and engraved in the glass in either red ink or blood stated, "Welcome, Robert." Robert knocked, but there was no answer. He rang the doorbell, and still had no answer. He took his baton and smashed one of the windows. He clambered inside and discovered it was dark, musty, and smelled like blood. He sprinted to the source of the smell. He opened the door and saw it was a cat that had been skinned! "Disgusting!" Robert whispered. As he closed the door, he remembered that he had a flashlight and turned it on. Click! He saw a door straight ahead of him. Robert kicked it open, and it revealed some basement stairs.

He slowly descended the stairs into a very creepy and unsettling basement. There was a large table with blood all over it. Robert then heard a voice. "I knew you would come." Robert spun around as he loaded the Spas-12. **KA-BANG!** Robert looked down. There in the man's arms lay Ava; he had killed her. The man was bleeding from his stomach. "My name is Cain Schizophrenia," the man said. Robert unloaded 5 more rounds on the man, and the man crumpled. However, he got up as if nothing had happened. He then said, "You were not careful. You got third." And with that, Cain drew a machete and slit Robert's throat. Robert was dead before he hit the floor.

Story IV

Runaway

This story is a realistic fiction that involves disappearances and trains. It takes place in Raleigh, NC, in the winter of 2011. The main character is a truck driver named Steven Lee, who is 28 years old. This story is filled with the unknown. In this story, who would expect a train to be the antagonist?

The day was quite dreary, the sky black with rain. Steven was heading to his job as a truck driver. The company he worked for delivered freight across distances under 300 miles. Steven was nearly running late when he was stopped at a train crossing as a train passed by. Fortunately, the train was short, and it only delayed Steven a minute. After arriving at his truck driving business, he checked in and viewed his schedule. There was an order for Gastonia, NC, for a large parcel of Amazon products that would only fit in the company's biggest truck. The price in return for the shipment was $500, which was oddly high! Steven booked the delivery and went over to the garage. He walked to the largest truck there, which was so large that it was kept in a separate garage. It required a special keycard, and the keycard was hard to obtain.

You had to have a certain number of working hours, be over 25 years old to drive, and the order must be for over $100, not including gas fees.

Steven drew the keycard from his lanyard and inserted it into the keycard slot in the door. He opened the door and headed to the truck's driver's side. Steven did not get to drive the truck as often as he liked, which made driving it all the more valuable. It had several new amenities, including a message radio, sunshades, and a smoother ride. After getting in, he transmitted the clearance codes to the operator located above the garage. The garage opened with the loud sound of the metal gears that supported it. Steven started the enormous machine and drove out of the garage with the loud roaring of the engines. He set off to a vast Amazon facility, which was about 15 minutes away, to pick up the goods at a cargo door. Once there, he called the cargo team, but oddly enough, there was no response. The store was tranquil; there was no one around.

At that moment, a man opened the door and said, "Hello. Sorry about the wait. The Admin was out sick today, so I was filling in." He gestured behind him. "Alright boys! Let's get to work!" A group of 4 men emerged, and they all started gathering boxes. The man who spoke to Steven said, "By the way, my name is Oliver. Oliver Smith." Steven asked, "Where is everyone? I expected more people at Amazon today."

Oliver said, "Ahh. Yes, that would be the strike going on! It's quite small, so it missed the papers, which is kind of convenient. Strikes are quite bad for business!" Steven responded, "That makes sense."

After the men packed all the boxes in the truck, Oliver bid Steven farewell saying, "Have a nice day." Steven started plotting his journey to Gastonia, which would take about 4 hours. He did not expect his trip to be interrupted just after it began. Fifteen minutes into the journey, Steven glanced to his left and saw a train going by the same track where the train had stopped him earlier that very morning. After staring for a little bit longer, he noticed something odd. The train was slowing down, which was uncommon through this area of Raleigh. He watched a little longer and realized something had crashed into the train! Steven looked and saw an optional U-turn at the light ahead.

When Steven got to the crossing, the train had nearly stopped, and it was blocking the crossing. Steven stopped his truck and saw what had crashed into the train; it was a now-totaled truck, which was sitting to the side of the tracks. He gasped; the truck was one of his company's smaller box trucks! Steven ran over to the driver's side of the truck and saw a woman trying to free herself from the seat belt. Steven reached into his belt and took out his pocket knife for emergencies. He cut the woman's seatbelt, and she stumbled out of the truck. After ensuring she was ok, Steven called 911 and informed them of the situation. The police asked him to go up to the train cab. Steven started running to the train cab, but it took much longer than he expected to reach the front of the train. When he got up to the train's engine, he found the train car pretty bumped up. He broke open a window and climbed in to check for any survivors.

There was just a small problem…there was not a single person on the train! It was not that they had all died when the train hit the truck, but the cabin was completely devoid of any human presence whatsoever! Steven looked around and searched for the train. He found nothing. He then tried to start up the train. Having some experience with trains, Steven radioed the train admin about the situation. Steven also informed him that the cab was deserted and that he knew how to drive the train. The train admin canceled the train route and asked Steven to back the train up at no faster than 15 miles per hour. Steven got to the wreck site a few minutes later, and the police, fire department, and medical services were already there. The police were baffled! They could not tell what had happened. It did not look like the train driver had fled when the train crashed into the truck. The police decided to put the case under investigation. The woman Steven saved had no significant injuries and thanked Steven profusely. However, there was no explanation for the disappearance of the train driver.

The remainder of Steven's trip to Gastonia was uneventful. After making a bathroom and lunch stop, he returned to the shipping company. The shipping company had already been informed of the train incident and forced the woman to pay over $50,000 in fees for the truck! Steven argued the case in court and helped to disperse the large sum of money between several sources. The only thing on the news for the next week was the peculiar train crash, and everyone in town was talking about it too. After about a week of normalcy, another abnormality happened.

Steven was on his way to work, and again the signal at the train tracks was red. Red on a train signal means no trains can go through that signal. In scarce instances, the operator allowed trains to go no faster than 15 miles per hour. Suddenly, the crossing arms started to lower. There was a train arriving, and Steven decided to look at the train. He mainly focused on the cab and saw that it did not have tempered glass; he could see clearly in the cab and saw that the train was completely devoid of life. Steven was shocked. He said aloud, "How can this happen again?!" He managed to get his phone in time to record the empty cab and the train going through the crossing much faster than 15 miles per hour. Once the crossing arms had gone back up, Steven started his car and called the police. "We will take it from here!" the police responded.

Steven took a short delivery this time at work, which was only 20 minutes away in Cary, NC. After returning from that delivery, the police officers requested the video he had captured of the train. It wasn't the best quality, but the police could make out that the cab was deserted. The police even got the F.B.I. to search for the train company responsible. According to the train company, a train wasn't scheduled until 30 minutes later! The F.B.I. was completely confused. "How can a train not be scheduled, and suddenly a train magically starts and doesn't stop?!" One F.B.I. member stated a significant fact that could end the great mystery. "Great Scott! Why didn't I think of this earlier?! We need to check the security cameras! If trains are starting without any explanation, then it could be a criminal who wants to cause chaos to be unleashed!" When he said this, everyone stared at the train commander. The train commander said, "I will check the cameras!"

Everyone accompanied him to the terminal at the top of the station center. The commander then shouted to one of his employees, "Drew! Could you please allow access to the video surveillance for the CCTV cameras at terminal B?" Drew replied, "Yes sir!" Everyone went through a glass door to the security room. The train commander pulled up the cameras. He said, "By the way, my name is Andrew." After Andrew pulled up the cameras, the F.B.I. commander sat down. The fast forwarded through the footage until, at 6:16 AM, a train started to pull out of the station. Not one person was in terminal B at the time. Everyone was shocked. The F.B.I. commander said, "We need to lock down all of terminal B." Andrew looked at the F.B.I. commander and said, "I will station myself by the entrance to ensure that not a single person tries to take control of a train." The F.B.I. commander said one last thing before departing. "We will also station a force of F.B.I. members by each entrance and exit here."

After the unexplained recording of the train reached the news stations, the story spread like wildfire. Life went on like normal for the next week for Steven. As he drove to work one day, he decided to check out the train tracks. Meanwhile, a set of tank cars started moving, but no one noticed. The F.B.I. agent assigned there was absent. The tank cars picked up speed. Steven examined the rail. It had a few markings on it. At that moment, Steven heard a noise which sounded like a set of train cars. Steven looked up in time to see the pair of tank cars right in front of him. **BANG!** Life for Steven seemingly disappeared in an instant.

Story V

Devoid of Luck

This story is a historical fiction story based on the horrific 9/11 attacks. This story is filled with unexpected suspense. The main character is in his late 20s, with a job as a CCTV camera operator and a technology specialist. His name is Jacob Smith. The date is August 12, 2001, and it takes place in New York City, NY.

"These computers have a mind of their own!" Jacob thought to himself. It had been a long day at work. Jacob was happy to go home to see his family. Sky, his wife, was the most wonderful lady on this earth! He even had a daughter named Charlotte that was just under a year old. Jacob arrived home from work at 6:00 PM, just in time for dinner; traffic had been bad on the subway. Sky worked as a banker in the North tower of the World Trade Center. They currently live on the outskirts of New York. However, this would change tomorrow when they moved into their new apartment. After they moved, their commute to work was cut from 25-35 minutes to 5-10 minutes! It was a bit of a chaotic night at the Smith's house. After they finished last-minute preparations for the move, Jacob and Sky went to bed.

The following day, Jacob and Sky went to work. Jacob noticed something odd about the workplace. It wasn't the workplace itself but the people. Everyone was avoiding him, but Jacob did not think much of it. When Jacob got home, however, he noticed that Sky had started to become shy towards him. Why was this, he wondered? Jacob did not think much of it. He dealt with this behavior for about a week and discovered it was only the beginning of many things going awry!

One day, he noticed his boss yelling at someone and taking his anger out on them. This was unnatural for his boss because his boss was normally calm. He also began to notice that Charlotte was unusually irritable. Jacob also noticed that the people he knew were growing more distant from him. Jacob was very startled by all of this! Everyone had a change in attitude that was very sudden. Things just didn't happen like this! The next day was even worse at work. The boss was mocking all of his employees! After another day, one of Jacob's co-workers decided that he had dealt with this long enough, and he went on strike! Jacob was worried. What was going on?! Could it just be a bad week? Or could this be because the stock market fell hundreds of points? Jacob did not think this was the case. "I just can't put my finger on it!" Jacob thought about all of this for a while and slept restlessly that night.

The next day, Jacob got into his car and drove to work as usual. However, there was a problem. The workplace was abandoned. Not a single person was there! Jacob searched for 30 minutes before finding a sign saying, "This workplace has been abandoned due to tax evasion." Jacob now had his answer. Aiden, his boss, was irritable because he was unable to pay taxes! Jacob got back into his car and headed home. Once home, he went upstairs to the newly installed attic, an amenity that his old home did not have. Jacob looked around in the gloomy crawlspace of the attic. Overall, it was pretty lonely. There was an assortment of items around the attic, including a desk and a journal with an old fountain pen. Jacob decided to check it out, and it was lucky he did! In it, he found a 20-dollar bill. He also found instructions on how to fold it.

"Turn to the side where Jackson's face is located and fold in half, similar to that of a hotdog. Go to the back side where The White House is. Fold this in half like a hamburger. The bill should be placed on the opposite side of the earth's gravitational pull. Fold each side where the middle crease is upward. Do the same with the other side. You now have a forecast of the very near future!"

Jacob wondered what "Forecast of the near future" meant. He looked at the folded bill and noticed something odd about it. It looked like a building was burning! He stared at it for a few more seconds before he noticed something. It wasn't a building; it was two buildings that were directly beside each other as they burned. Jacob stared at the bill for a little longer before he noticed that the buildings were here in New York. They were the twin towers! Jacob stumbled backward in fright and landed on the attic floor. **Creeeeek**! The attic floor collapsed beneath Jacob! Jacob fell through the floor and awoke to find himself in the hospital. He was there for several days but was finally able to return home from the hospital at 8:00 AM on September 11, 2001. During his stay in the hospital, he had no contact with his wife, Sky.

The first thing Jacob did when he got out of the hospital was trying to warn Sky. However, when he got to his house, Sky wasn't there! She had already gone to work, and Jacob did not get to warn her about the message found with the money! **KA-BOOM!!!** Jacob heard a loud sound coming from the street shortly after he got home. He wondered if it was a gunshot…or a bomb. It was neither! People were shouting that a plane had flown directly into the North Tower! It was the tower that Sky was in! Jacob ran to his car and drove as close as he could get to the North Tower. When he got there, all he could see was chaos. The first responders had a terrible time getting to the survivors. Jacob headed inside the burning North Tower, but when he got inside, he was met with a group of people trying to get out.

The air smelled of burning metal and rubber. Jacob was able to make it to the stairwell. He was up at least 12 stories when Jacob heard another ear-splitting **KA-BOOM!** He felt the tower shake! The South Tower had been hit just 20 minutes after the North Tower had been hit! This could not have been an ordinary plane crash. It had to be something more! Jacob kept sprinting past people when he heard the ear-splitting and gut-wrenching sound of metal splitting. The South tower was collapsing! A first responder asked him to leave the building immediately. Jacob ignored her and pushed forward! Finally, 30 minutes later, he found Sky! He hugged her, and they started to leave the building. Just as they were about to do so, there was an enormous shaking throughout the building! The North tower was collapsing! Jacob and Sky went down with the building like so many others, posing no significance in the world whatsoever!

Story VI

The Facility

This story is based on one of my YouTube videos! You can find the full movie at the link below this text. The main character is a prisoner of war forced to go to a secret government facility, but this is no ordinary facility! This is a science fiction facility with monsters and creatures that will haunt you until the ends of the earth. It takes place in 1991, and the main character's name is Steve Black.[11]

BANG! The sound of Spas-12 shotguns reverberated in the air as it decimated the enemy! It was one of the great Oil Wars! The Oil Wars have been going on for a while now. Steve is a US delegate. **BANG-BANG-BANG!** Steve shot his Desert Eagle into an oncoming enemy. Steve shouted, "Keep up the assault!" The small delegation of US troops pushed forward. They were met with a surprisingly small amount of resistance. **KA-BOOM!** There was a tank at 12 o'clock! Their general shouted, "**Fallback! Fallback!**" However, this had no impact! Steve did not notice the

---

[11]https://www.youtube.com/watch?v=jTF7huRP5T4&t=1s

tank focusing on a patch of ground just 2 feet ahead of him. **KA-BOOM!** The tank fired, knocking Steve unconscious. The rest of the army surrendered. They lost just one of many battles of the great Oil War!

When Steve woke up, he discovered he was in a hospital, hooked up to multiple wires and tubes. A doctor came in to check on him. "Mr. Black, you are awake." The doctor checked his notes. "You might be discouraged to know that the United States lost the battle." Steve replied, "Well, what exactly are you going to do with me now?" The doctor said, "This is an inconclusive victory since the general signed a treaty that states that for our oil, we can have the remaining US soldiers participate in government testing." Steve responded, "Ok…so what do I need to do?" The doctor responded, "You will be transported to the government facility in a few hours." Before the doctor left, he said, "Oh, by the way, the facility tests biological monstrosities. Your instructor will tell you about the procedures. 100 soldiers will be going. Good luck. You will need it!" The doctor left the room and was replaced by a trooper with a P90 and tactical gear. He escorted Steve outside, where the other soldiers had gathered. About fifteen minutes later, they were taken to the airport, where they had each taken a seat on the plane. They were off on a journey that would change their lives forever!

They arrived at the government facility at 4:00 PM. Its logo had a weird circle with arrows pointed to the center that read **SCP: SECURE CONTAIN PROTECT**. The soldiers escorted Steve inside, where even more soldiers greeted them. He waited a bit longer until the area overseer arrived. "Hello," he said, "you are prisoners of war. This is your home now. You will be known as Class-D personnel. Class-D personnel are to go with scientists and conduct experiments on the strange anomalies of this facility. The vast majority of anomalies are dangerous! Some are safe, but even if they are classified as safe, that does not mean they are not fatal. You do not need any further explanation currently. The MTF units will escort you to your cells. MTF stands for Mobile Task Force. They have the right to exterminate any resistance if need be! Good luck. And most importantly, don't die!"

The overseer left, and the rest of the newly appointed Class-D personnel were escorted through a long series of hallways. They were forced to change into inmate-like garments with "Class-D" stamped on the back, along with a number. Steve's number was 2173. The next day was the start of testing. Steve was lucky to have a nice MTF unit escort him to his first test subject, which was named SCP-914. The MTF unit gave him a slip of paper and a few everyday household items. The SCP was a weird clockwork-looking machine. On the paper, it instructed Steve to put one item in one slot, and another item would come out of the other slot. The class of the object was safe.

Steve went inside and set the first item down. The first item was a glass Coke bottle. He went over to the machine's control panel. He flipped a switch. **VRRRRR-CRRRRR!** The machine sprang to life, and the two doors closed. A few seconds later, the doors opened, and the glass bottle had vanished to be replaced with some salt and a lightbulb! Steve was instructed to give the items to the MTF unit there. He continued this process with the items until an announcement came over the loudspeaker. "Attention: the cafeteria is now open for food. Please make your way to the cafeteria at this time." The announcement ended, and the MTF unit escorted Steve to the cafeteria and allowed him to get some breakfast. The food was average, nothing too special. When Steve finished eating, he was escorted back to SCP-914. Steve worked with the SCP all day before ending his shift.

Nothing much happened the first month that Steve was at the facility. He met a new friend named Fred Akuji, who was intent on escaping the facility. The United States was less than 2000 miles away, and Canada was even closer! However, Steve noticed that the conditions were not the best. Since they were war veterans, the 100 soldiers were exceptionally equipped to handle the harshness of the facility, but that did not mean that the SCPs could not harm the soldiers. Two men had been killed by the monsters when the facility made that mistake! At that point, Steve realized he was sleeping in a dead man's bed.

A month after moving to the facility, Steve was redirected to a different SCP called SCP-049. SCP-049 was a much harder SCP to deal with. For one, it was not labeled under the "Safe" category. SCP-049 had the appearance of a plague doctor. Steve was instructed that SCP-049 was very dangerous, and he was to escort SCP-049 to different parts of the facility. SCP-049 would be flanked with at least 2 MTF units, and it would be caged up when transported due to being so hard to contain.

There are different classes for SCPs. The first SCP that Steve tested was classified as "Safe," and SCP-049 was classified as "Euclid" due to being more dangerous. After Steve was informed of everything, the MTF units caged SCP-049 up, and Steve started leading SCP-049 with lavender. No one knew why, but SCP-049 liked lavender. So people could infer that if SCP-049 liked lavender, he could be a plague doctor, since in the 14th century, they used it to stop the spread of the bubonic plague! What people soon figured out was that SCP-049 was multilingual. He could speak multiple languages, but the ones he spoke most were English and Medieval French.

Steve was escorted to the cell of SCP-049, and he waited outside the heavy blast doors. "The pestilence is inner." Steve heard this coming from the door, and the words sent shivers down his spine! SCP-049 looked precisely like a plague doctor from Medieval Europe. SCP-049 turned to Steve and said, "I can sense it!" Steve stared in horror at the creature. What did it mean? What could make sense? Steve did not have long to dwell on this due to the MTF units directing him to walk with SCP-049. The walk was pretty uneventful. SCP-049 seemed pretty compliant. After walking to the biochemistry lab, SCP-049 was given a series of interesting and indescribable tests. After what seemed like forever, the MTF units returned with SCP-049, and Steve was instructed to lead SCP-049 back to its cell with lavender. However, as they were approaching the cell, an announcement came onto the loudspeakers. "Attention all Mobile Task Force units, there is a rogue Class-D unit in the cafeteria. The Class-D unit is heavily armed! We need all available MTF units in the area to go to the cafeteria immediately!" The three MTF units that had accompanied Steve and the SCP to the cell locked SCP-049 in and ran to the cafeteria, which was only a short distance away. **BANG!** The sound of a gun fire echoed in the air. Steve sprinted to where it had originated from. The MTF units neutralized the rogue Class-D. It was Fred Akuji. He was dead.

The next few days were full of nothing but the talk of Fred. However, as the days wore on, the discussions of Steve's friend died down to almost nothing. Steve was able to find the statistics of how many were dead. Along with Fred, there were 5 soldiers dead from SCPs. Over the next week, Steve noticed that people were on edge. Something was off! It was not the prisoners that were on edge, it was the higher-ranking officials. Even the 05-Command seemed worried! Steve wondered what the cause of their worry was, but he did not need to wait long to find out. He had his answer the following week. The United States had located the prisoners, and they would be rescued! The prisoners were excited. One day when Steve was in the cafeteria, he heard a muffled explosion reverberating from deep in the facility. Everyone looked in the direction of the noise; they all started talking and moving restlessly when they heard the sound of weapons being fired. Despite the noise of the Class-D inmates, Steve was able to make out the loudspeaker announcement. "Attention all MTF units and Class-D personnel…we are under attack! All MTF units report to Gate A **NOW!** All Class-D personnel, please head back to your cells to ensure your safety and the safety of others!"

The announcement ended and everyone went back to their cells. Once everyone was in the cell containment center, an MTF unit closed the heavy blast door and locked the inmates in. Everyone heard gunfire for what seemed like forever until they heard a voice from the door shouting **STAY BACK**! Everyone moved out of the way of the door. **KA-BANG!** The door exploded with the force of a small bomb and several US Army members charged in. One of the soldiers then said into his walkie-talkie, "Army members acquired!" The soldiers escorted the Class-D units outside to 5 boats; they were met with little resistance. The Army then sailed back to a larger ship off the coast. The US Army questioned all the ex-inmates about the SCP facility. The US army was not too worried since the island belonged to Canada.

After sorting things out, they gave the troopers bottles of water and then asked everyone if they wanted to go to an SCP facility in Maine. Most agreed, and about a month later, the US sorted everything out. Several people chose to go to Maine and work at the SCP facility. The US had 8 people become scientists and 5 to become Mobile Task Force units. Steve was one of the 8 scientists that made the cut. He was assigned to tend after one of the most dangerous monsters in the facility! Its ID was SCP-096.

You could tell that SCP-096 was challenging to deal with because the security measures were insane! A five-meter cube of airtight steel was his cage. Pressure sensors and laser detectors were in place, and no photos or videos were permitted of SCP-096. It's no wonder why these security measures are in place! SCP-096 measures about 2.38 meters or over seven and a half feet in height! Not only that, but its jaw can open 4 times the average size of any human, it can jump insane distances, and run upwards of 25 miles per hour! The skeleton of SCP-096 is nearly invincible, and it can survive without organs and blood. SCP-096 is usually in a docile state. However, if you look into its eyes, it will become agitated. It will then proceed to break anything in its path until it can get to the person that saw its eyes and kill them! SCP-096 may be the most difficult SCP in this area, but Steve approached this challenge without fear.

Steve is walking to the containment center where he will test the cage's strength. Overnight, SCP-096 was moved to another part of the facility. Once Steve got past all of the security, he was given several types of guns to test the strength of the containment area. He tested what felt like a full arsenal of firearms against the same wall for hours. He did some other cell containment tasks for the next two weeks before he was tasked to move SCP-096 back to the cage. Steve was heading down the hallway toward SCP-096 and was making the last turn before the cafeteria emerged into view when the unexpected happened. **POP!** All of the lights went out! Everyone jumped up in a panic! Steve took out a flashlight and started running to where the containment chamber for SCP-096 should be. However, when he opened the door, it was missing! Steve got a notification on his radio telling him that he needed to be at a specific location. Steve sprinted to the area and discovered he was accidentally misled into going to a different part of the facility. SCP-096 was locked in a cube, and no less than 14 MTF units accompanied SCP-096 to its cell.

After securing SCP-096, Steve walked back toward his living quarters. The lights flickered and were turned back on. An announcement then bellowed throughout the hallways saying, "Power has been restored to the facility. Thank you for your cooperation." Steve continued walking until the alarm started to go off! The announcement stated, "A highly dangerous SCP has escaped and is roaming the hallways! SCP-096 is out of its containment chamber! All available MTF units to Sector B now! **I repeat! All MTF units to sector B NOW!**" Steve stopped for a moment before running to his living quarters. He quickly grabbed a gun from one of his racks. It was a silencer-equipped M1A4 with armor-piercing bullets. He also grabbed a Glock 17 and an armor vest and then ran back out the door. Even though he was not assigned to go there, he wanted to help.

At that very moment, however, another announcement rang through the facility and the alarms stopped. "SCP-096 has been secured. All personnel are now dismissed. There have been 3 casualties. Please come to the 05 office if you are contacted about the deaths." Steve did not receive any notifications that day, until after dinner. It stated, "Please come to the 05 office. You are being assigned to another SCP." Steve made his way to the office but stopped to get a glazed creme-filled doughnut on the way there. He enjoyed the savory morsels of the SCP facilities' doughnuts as he made his way to the office.

Steve arrived at the 05-command center at about 9:00 pm. It was pitch black outside due to a storm. Steve knocked on the door, and it was opened by none other than Dr. Banes. Banes owned the SCP facility. Steve had never met Banes before. He was an impressive man at seven feet tall! He was 49, soon to be 50, on December 29th. Steve greeted the towering man a little hesitantly and entered the room. Banes then said, "We have been expecting you. Would you like a cup of tea and maybe some biscuits?" Having not known that the doctor was British, Steve was a little surprised. Steve nodded yes in reply. Dr. Banes said, "Please, take a seat, Steve Black."

Steve sat down, and all of them discussed work and logistics. Steve was getting bored and asked, "Banes, you brought me here to switch which SCP monsters we test on. Could we please discuss this?" Banes replied, "Yes, of course! Sorry, I am very social…ah…sometimes too social! But yes, of course. What SCP did you have in mind?" Steve responded, "Well, I was thinking of one of the oldest, if not the oldest SCP in this facility. I think SCP-173 would be a good pick." Steve glanced at the detailed clock on the mantelpiece. It read November 22, 1994. Below it was a clock stating that the time was 9:39 pm.

A loud exclamation from Dr. Banes brought his attention back to the subject. "Ah! Yes, of course! My favorite and least favorite monster, SCP-173!" Banes said, "I would like to tell you the story of how I was able to obtain SCP-173. 81 years ago, a ship called the Greyrock sank. My friend made a replica of the Greyrock in 1964 and had several others join us for a voyage. We had exquisite food to eat and comfortable beds. We even had a phonograph! However, that did not stop it from sinking. One of my friends had the location of SCP-173. I escaped the sinking, and we were able to get to SCP-173 quickly. The rest is history!"

When Dr. Banes had finished talking, the room erupted in applause. Banes grinned and said, "Thank you! Thank you!" After most of the biscuits were finished, Steve brought up a question. "What is SCP-173 like? If you are going to let me work with it, shouldn't I know the workings of SCP-173?" Banes replied, "Yes. SCP-173 is the class of Euclid, and for good reason. SCP-173 needs to be locked in a special container at all times and no fewer than 3 personnel must enter at a time. The door must be locked for obvious reasons that I will get to in a little bit. At least 2 MTF units need to make eye contact with SCP-173 until everyone has vacated the scene. SCP-173 is extremely hostile, and a direct line of sight must not be broken. SCP-173 can't move if observed within a direct line of sight. SCP-173 will even attack you if no one is watching it. And how it attacks is spine-chilling...literally! You see, it attacks by snapping the neck at the base of the skull! I think that is all you need to know at this time."

Steve loved the idea and prospect of working with SCP-173. Thus, he took the job. He had a few assignments this week and completed all but two. It had been 13 weeks since the Oil Wars. Steve walked to the cell with 5 other MTF units. Sweat is forming on Steve's forehead; he is quite anxious! If his line of sight is broken even for a blink of an eye, he is a dead man! **Ru-RRRRRRRRRR-Cr!** The door slid open. Steve had seen SCP-173 multiple times, but it was still terrifying! Steve had everyone maintain eye contact with the horrific monster. Steve walked forward with a high-tech element finder. Steve put the finder about a foot away from SCP-173. It picked up a mix of elements, including concrete and rebar.

He now advanced to the most dangerous part...the head. It picked up Krylon brand spray paint, of all things! Steve backed away slowly. He then said to the MTF units, "Let's go." Steve let two MTF units watch SCP-173 while another signaled to a guard to close the doors. Steve signaled to close the door, and the two MTF units backed away. The mission had been a success, and Steve was relieved! He only had one more assignment this week: to escort a few inmates or Class-D personnel to SCP-173 as test subjects. He was ready!

The next day, Steve got dressed quickly. It was nearly 3:00 AM. Steve walked a short distance to the cells of Class-D 1137, 2495, and 3008. He walked them to the housing chamber of SCP-173. After handing them a paper about SCP-173, they walked in. Steve walked up to the guard and took his place. He tried to close the door, but it did not work. Steve said to the inmates, "Uhh, there seems to be a problem with the door control system. Please maintain direct eye contact with SCP-173!" Steve was worried. He knew a simple accident could result in an entire containment breach! Steve loaded his gun. He then heard the snapping of necks and blood splattering. Steve thought, "Darn!" and half-shouted to the only Class-D alive, "Please back away from SCP-173!" The Class-D did so. The power flickered. At that very moment, SCP-173 moved to where Steve was standing. Steve let out a shriek that was cut short by SCP-173. **CRACK!** Steve collapsed to the ground. He was dead. [12]

---

[12] https://scp-wiki.wikidot.com/scp-914
https://scp-wiki.wikidot.com/scp-049
https://scp-wiki.wikidot.com/scp-096
https://scp-wiki.wikidot.com/scp-173

Story VII

Lights

This story is based on a Roblox horror game called Welcome. The video is on my YouTube channel. Welcome was created by Dexus Studios. The character's name is Edgar Cross, and the story took place in 1952. Without further ado, I welcome you to a tale of suspense and mystery.[13]

It was an ordinary rainy night in November. Edgar was driving home from the grocery store. He had been there for too long and needed to get home. After a long day of work, Edgar was a sleep-deprived zombie! When Edgar stepped foot inside his home, he set down the groceries in the cabinet and lit a candle. The house did not have much power, being over half a century old. **PING!** The sound of a light bulb breaking reached Edgar's ears. Edgar fell around in the darkness in search of glass shards. He found the fragments and nearly scratched himself.

_____

[13] https://youtu.be/ncAnQXlIjz4

Now that he knew where the light had broken, he reached around the kitchen's granite countertop into the pantry. The house belonged to a couple from Germany that had died due to lead poisoning. Edgar wondered if the house was haunted. He shrugged. He doubted that the ghosts of the previous owners haunted the house. Edgar knew the renovators had placed a bulb in the pantry because of the power shortage and faulty wires. Edgar focused his candle on the wall of the pantry. On the back wall, he found a spare bulb. He grabbed it and screwed it into the lamp with the demolished lightbulb. Edgar suddenly felt dizzy, and he fainted! When he woke up, he immediately noticed that the power was out. "Funny," Edgar said with a bitter tone. He supposed it might have been a breaker. The breaker was very old.

Edgar walked over to a door beside the pantry and opened it. He took a flashlight and flipped the lever to turn on the breaker. Edgar started walking towards his bed, but at that very moment, there was an enormous banging sound. Edgar was startled by the noise and began walking toward the sound, but at that moment, he noticed something walking on the balcony upstairs! Edgar was very disturbed! He lived alone. How could a person get in without him noticing? Edgar decided he should call the police. There was a phone in the dining room that Edgar used. He dialed 911, but the call would not pick up. Edgar turned around, and the lights flickered and died for the second time that night.

Across from the phone, Edgar saw a pair of luminescent red eyes staring at him! Suddenly, the eyes disappeared.

Edgar headed again to the breaker room, but when he got there to turn the electricity back on, the door was locked! He knew he hadn't locked the door behind him. There was another breaker box in the basement. He went to his bedroom to get the basement key and unlocked the basement door. Edgar turned on the power and looked around. He noticed a large hole in the wall that had not been there the last time he had been in the basement. It was boarded up. He needed to find a way to tear down the boards. He went back up the basement stairs and into the garage. On one of the shelves, there sat a crowbar. Edgar picked it up, and then the most unexpected thing occurred. The car alarm went off! Edgar was quite startled! He ran quickly out of the garage and slammed the door. Sweat was accumulating on Edgar's forehead, and he was breathing hurriedly.

After pulling himself together, Edgar descended to the basement, where he hacked away at the screws holding the boards. After tearing them down, he could walk through the hole in the wall, which led to a hallway. What happened next made Edgar's heart stop! A creepy spider-like being crawled down the wall and then out of sight! Edgar thought he was hallucinating when it disappeared. It did not reappear. Instead, once

Edgar got to the end of the hallway, he was met with a room full of red demon-like figures appearing all around the room! Edgar blinked, and they were gone. Edgar said to the empty room, "Thank goodness I was only hallucinating!" He noticed a door on the other side of the room. It needed a code for it to open. Edgar contemplated, "How much of this house do I not know about?!" He decided right then that he would move the very next day and sue the renovators of the house! Edgar made his way upstairs and started searching everywhere for the code. As he got to the top of the stairwell, a figure darted around Edgar and went past where Edgar would have been standing if not for his good reflexes! What on earth was happening, he wondered?

Edgar made his way to the workshop. He unlocked the door, and as he opened the door and stepped foot inside the workshop, everything around him turned a bright neon red! It then reverted to the colors of the house. He noticed a map at the back of the room. At this point, Edgar started to worry for his sanity! He picked up the map. To summarize, it stated that Edgar needs to look at the map and enter the code that corresponds to the first letter of every city on the map. The cities in order are Stanmord, Aystar, Tramore, Aurele, and Nasville. Interestingly, the last city sounded a lot like Nashville!

The code turned out to be SATAN! Satan is the leader of all things evil! Edgar noticed an article with the map. It was written in 1946. "That's it!" Edgar thought. That was the door code! 1946! Edgar made his way down to the basement and punched the code in. It worked! Edgar made his way down another hallway that led to a maze. He made his way down the maze, and Edgar thought he was on to something. However, at that moment, a creature started following Edgar! The beast was a mangled mess of blood and skin and had 6 spider-like legs! Edgar screamed and started running. He was not looking where he was going and fell; he never stopped falling. Edgar stared at the blankness ahead of him. It was magenta. A voice told him that his house was located between the shadow realm, essentially in a portal of monsters! The voice instructed him to obtain 3 orbs, and all of the madness would cease. A woman named Algiz explained everything and helped him search for the orbs. Edgar had already collected one orb from falling through it. Algiz led him to the second and third ones. However, after finding the third one, Algiz disappeared to be replaced by the spider figure, and it then knocked Edgar out!

Edger woke up 2 days later in a prison surrounded by dead and mangled corpses! He screamed, and it took 10 minutes for him to calm down! After finally controlling himself, Edgar discovered he could walk out of the prison to his house. As he walked into his house, he saw that all the items in his house were completely flipped upside down! Even though Edgar questioned the reality of his life, he continued. He immediately noticed it was cold and decided to turn on the fireplace. The fireplace was surprisingly not upside down, and neither was his table, which now had a weird symbol on it.

Once Edgar turned on the fireplace, the TV turned on of its own accord. A voice on the TV said, "I am searching. I am looking. I am finding. You must find what belongs to me!" Candles suddenly appeared in a pathway leading to someplace. Edgar inferred that he needed to find the symbols like the ones on the table. Edgar searched for a while until he had every last one. After that, he received a code and went through a maze. After completing the maze, Edgar entered a house. The house then began to shake. The spider figure appeared and shouted, "**GIVE ME YOUR SOUL!**" The demons feasted joyously that night.

Story VIII

Blankless Void

This story is a realistic fiction story that is based on the popular game called "Among Us." This story takes place in the future, and our main character, whose name is Alex Croft, is one of many going to colonize the planet Mars. However, there is something amiss. All of their plans spontaneously go awry due to the presence of a murderer on the ship!

"Breaking news! SpaceX is launching Amaryllis on May 4, 2063! Only one a week away! All letters have been sent to the astronauts, who will be leaving soon!" Click! Alex turned off the TV. He got up from the couch and started preparing dinner. He was single and lived alone. He earned $150,000 each year working at SpaceX. He did not think that a launch letter would be sent to him. He looked around at his house. He was able to pay it off in a few years. He was 22 years old, and it was highly improbable that Elon Musk would hire him for the mission. As Alex was contemplating, there was a click of the doorbell. Alex had an LED light and speaker setup that activated whenever someone rang the doorbell. The Imperial March would play, and the lights would sync to the music.

Alex opened the door to a finely dressed individual. Alex greeted the man by saying, "Hello. What can I do for you?" The man said nothing in reply but instead handed Alex a letter. Alex glanced at the letter, and then looked up. The man had disappeared. Alex shut the door, went inside, and opened the letter.

Dear Dr. Croft,

We are pleased to inform you that you have been accepted into the program, Amaryllis! We know you have only been working here a few months, but we have seen expert growth in knowledge, and we would like for you to take part in the colonization of Mars! You will need to be at the SpaceX launch site at 516. This is T-60:00 before launch. The rocket will then be directed to The Discovery. The Discovery will transport you and 14 others to Mars in about 3 weeks. You are required to complete this mission. Please bring only items you will need for 45 minutes of flight time. Everything else will be provided. Thank you for your time!

Yours sincerely, Elon Musk

Alex stared at the letter in amazement as he digested the info. He yelled, "**YAHOO!**" He then prepared his things for work tomorrow. He set his alarm to wake him at 4:00 AM and went to bed.

The following day, Alex got dressed and drove to the launch pad of SpaceX. He counted 15 cars. Alex walked to the meeting room. Elon Musk was there and discussed the plans for the adventure. After prepping them, all 15 astronauts headed to the largest rocket in the world, the Amaryllis. It had nearly 100 million pounds of thrust behind it! It could reach a top speed of 10,000 miles per hour on earth. In space, its speed could reach 105,000 miles per hour! After making some final decisions, everyone was in the rocket. The cabin was pretty spacious. The captain of the rocket then put in the coordinates for The Discovery, and the countdown began. Launch in T-30 seconds! Ten, nine, eight, seven, six, five, four, three, two, one, liftoff! The noise was deafening, but the launch was a success!

During the 45-minute ride in the rocket, Alex started up a conversation with one of the crew members. Her name was Emma. She was quite nice and talked about her life. She was 21 years old, which made her the youngest on the trip. After docking with The Discovery, everyone was shown to their rooms. Recently added features were pressurized cabins and gravitational pull. The ship looked a lot like a futuristic home! The rooms were also fitted with personal customizations. The captain called a meeting after everything was sorted out with the rooms. Once everyone was there, the captain addressed them by saying, "Hello. My name is John. I am your captain for this mission. I hope you are comfortable in your environment because we will be here for three weeks before we reach Mars!"

Everyone talked for a while about statistics. Once they were done discussing, everyone went to the cafeteria for breakfast. Alex sat beside Emma and began to share some of his life stories. "I was born on April 25, 2041. My parents are alive and well. We went to a local church and were very sociable. When I was 13, I started to struggle with depression. That depression continues to this day. I was at the top of my class, and one day, I took an intelligence test and proved to everyone that I had an IQ of 141! I also got into SCP stuff when I was around 14. I wrote a book, but I did not achieve popularity. I was betrayed by my best friend when I was 15, and my next best friend died in a rogue car."

At this point, Alex had tears falling from his eyes like raindrops. Emma reached over and patted him on the back. Emma replied to the tragic story by saying, "I am so sorry that you had to go through that! I went through something similar with my boyfriend! One day, Allen left my house, and I never saw him again. He did not answer my texts. Another boyfriend died! You know what…I don't want to talk about that. Sorry! I also struggle with depression and anxiety. I want you to know that you are not alone!" When

Emma had finished speaking, Alex got himself together and said, "Thank you! I needed to let all my emotions out and share my story!" At that moment, another fellow astronaut approached the table and said, "Hello! My name is Ryan. Can I join you?" Emma and Alex both nodded, and Ryan pulled up a chair.

From the first few minutes of talking with Ryan, Alex could tell that Ryan was an extrovert because he just kept on talking and asking questions. "I am from Britain, and I was a music composer before I began working for SpaceX." Ryan then paused. "Emma and I have been good friends for a few years now. We have had our fair share of memories!" Ryan talked with them for another hour and then left for his room. Alex checked his watch and exclaimed, "Great Scott! Ryan talked for over an hour!" Emma told him, "Oh, you will get used to Ryan after a while!" Alex nodded and replied, "I suppose so." Captain John approached the two and said, "Hello. The ship needs a little fine-tuning to be fully operational, and you could honestly use the workload! Alex, do you mind taking out the trash on the ship?" Alex replied, "Of course, I don't mind!" John nodded and turned to Emma. "Do you mind taking care of the wiring?" Emma replied, "You got it!" John then said, "Thanks to you both. Have a nice day!"

As John was walking away, Alex decided to create a pun. "What if we hadn't taken those tasks? Would you have wished us a bad day?" John turned around and shook his head. John grinned and said to Alex, "I can't believe I'm stuck with you for 3 weeks!" Alex let out a loud laugh that seemed to shake the entire ship. He started gathering up the trash and hauled it to an area on the ship where waste is disposed of in space. Alex opened the hatch and tossed it in the trash with an audible **THUMP!** Alex closed the hatch and opened the vacuum seal. After disposing of the waste, he went to the fitness center at the end of The Discovery. He worked out for a few hours and had lunch.

After lunch, Alex Face Timed with his family and played chess with Emma, who beat him solidly. Alex then decided to bring up his life story again. "Hey, I don't believe I finished telling my life story, so can I continue telling you about it?" Emma stopped playing chess and said, "Sure." Alex smiled and then proceeded with his story. "After the friend drama, I had PTSD and had suicidal thoughts for a while before deciding that I should stay on this earth…or universe I should say. When I was 17, I asked Jesus into my heart and was baptized. I also went to college 2 years later, bringing my story to where I am now." Emma said, "Nice! You have a cool life story. I would rather not share mine because…I know I will cry if I start talking about it!" Alex and Emma talked some more, and Alex watched some internet broadcasts. Before they even realized it, it was dinner time.

Alex and Emma talked a little bit at dinner, and then everyone began to head to their rooms for bed. As they left the cafeteria area, John pulled Alex aside. John said to him, "Listen. I don't know if you can tell, but everyone is on edge, and I don't know why! Nothing is going wrong, but I just need you to be wary of the crew!" Alex stared at John. "Ok. But what makes you so sure?" Alex asked. John responded, "It's hard to explain!" Alex sighed and said, "Well, I just hope nothing is amiss. Goodnight, sir!" Alex left the cafeteria and headed to his room to go to sleep.

The following day, Alex was awoken by a blood-curdling scream and several shouts! It took Alex a few seconds before realizing what was happening. He hurried to his closet, put on his clothes, and ran outside. What met him there sent shivers down his spine! There was a fellow astronaut whose body was covered in a silvery color of foreign blood mixed with red blood! He was dead! Alex was quite startled when he heard footsteps behind him. It was Emma. She let out an audible gasp. John came sprinting around the corner of the hallway. When John came into sight of the body, he said, "Who did this?!" He looked around. No one knew. John examined the body. "He is dead." John studied the body some more. "This is no ordinary cut. This is a bite! Look at the teeth marks! The bite broke his neck and broke bones C4-C7." John stood up, dragged the body to a trash bag, and ejected it outside. John then trapped the body and brought it back inside. The body was completely frozen. John vacuum-sealed it and put it in a special storage container.

That day, everyone spoke in whispers. The next few days were pretty uneventful, but 2 days after all of the chaos that occurred, something else happened. When Alex went to check the cameras, he saw a dead body! Alex swallowed hard and ran to John's quarters. Alex hammered on the door. John opened the door hurriedly in his night clothes and followed Alex to the body. The body was completely severed in half! The severed end laid 5 feet away. The same cutting pattern was apparent almost at once. John called a meeting, and after he informed everyone of everything that had happened, they all started freaking out! No one slept that night. Three days passed without any more dead bodies.

Alex was walking to the arcade when he suddenly heard something; it sounded like a slow drip of something. At that moment, Alex also felt a hand on his ankle. He spun around and screamed a horrible scream! A scream of mortal terror! It was Ryan. He was dead. He had been stabbed 6 times! Another astronaut was there with Ryan, and he had also been stabbed 6 times. Alex ran to get John from his living quarters. John ran to the bodies and froze them. He then called another meeting. Most of the team was crying, with Emma crying the hardest. An astronaut named Drew, and three others, were not crying. Alex put one arm around Emma's shoulder. After assessing the body details and contacting the family members, they had dinner. Everyone was quiet and reserved. Alex talked to Emma for several hours over dinner about Ryan. After many tears were shed for Ryan, everyone went to bed. Probably more accurately, everyone laid down in their beds, trying to go to sleep but not being able to push away the thought of ending up like Ryan. Everyone wondered if they would be next. The night was even darker than usual.

There were no deaths for a week. According to John, there was only a week left on the trip! However, that also meant that there were 11 people still alive. Alex was sleeping when a knock on the door awoke him. Alex reached for his pajamas and put on his shirt and pants. He also grabbed a sharp iron rod from his bedside table because he had no idea what was behind the door! Luckily, it was only Emma. "I couldn't sleep and…I just really need a friend to talk to." Alex led her inside to a couch and gave her a blanket and made a steaming mug of hot cocoa. Emma proceeded to ask about how home life was for Alex and about his faith. It turns out that both Emma and Alex were Christians. After talking for a while, Alex and Emma prayed for the killer or killers, that they would stop killing people and see the error of their ways.

After finishing the prayer, they heard a noise. **THUMP!** Alex and Emma turned to the noise, and both ran to the door with a look of sheer terror on their faces! Alex opened the door and spotted another dead body, this time with no blood. He concentrated more on the footsteps growing fainter from the crime scene. Alex shouted to Emma, "Stay here!" He started running. The sound of the footsteps increased. Alex didn't notice them stop until it was too late! **SHINK!** The blade of a knife sunk into Alex's shoulder! Alex hollered out in pain. He couldn't make out who the murderer was. However, the murderer did not kill Alex. He ran away. Alex then blacked out.

A day later, Alex awoke in a hospital bed. The knife had only minorly injured his shoulder. Once Alex was able to leave his bed, everyone had a meeting. Alex informed them of what had happened, and they all suspected that Drew was the murderer. Drew seemed very confused, but all the evidence pointed to him. Drew was sent out into the endless space. A day passed with no deaths. Alex overheard two people talking. One voice said, "Are you doing well? I haven't seen you much. Might be good and bad in this scenario." The second voice said, "Well, with the murders I committed, I'm doing just fine!" Alex ran to John's living quarters to inform him, and once again, John hosted a meeting. No one believed Alex except for Emma. Alex was shocked! It's not like they thought that he was the killer. They just thought that he imagined things or something. Two days passed. Alex wanted to view the security cameras, but when he tried to get on, he noticed the signal had been jammed! Alex decided to walk to the electricity center and turn on the server.

At that moment, he heard footsteps behind him. He pretended to "work" on the cameras and reached for a wrench. Alex spun around and knocked the knife out of the person's hand; the wrench made contact with the person's skull with a resounding **THUD!** Alex was losing the fight until a pair of hands reached behind the killer and held him back long enough so Alex could knock him out with the wrench. The person who had helped Alex defeat the killer was Emma. John rounded the corner and cuffed the killer. John, of course, announced an emergency meeting. The killer was voted to be launched out into space. He met his doom. Alex, Emma, and the rest of the crew dispersed. However, another dead body was found! John alerted the crew that someone else had died. This left only 9 people still alive!

While the group was meeting, the scariest and most unexpected thing happened. An asteroid hit! The lights flickered, and people went to the cannons to deflect any other asteroids from contacting the ship. Everyone was lucky to survive. No major damage had been done to the ship. Another day passed. Alex was walking by the cafeteria when a resounding explosion occurred.

Alex ran to the source of the blast. Emma was already working on it when a figure came up behind Emma. Alex yelled, "**NO!**" as he rushed forward to knock the killer off balance. Dan was the killer, and after Alex knocked him off balance, Dan got up and ran. Just then, another explosion came from the reactor. Alex decided to help Emma fix the reactor. They informed John, who ordered an emergency meeting to take place. Despite the evidence, the voting was skewed. Dan voted for Alex, 4 people voted for Emma, and 4 people voted for Dan. Since no one could decide who the killer was, everyone dispersed again. Two dead bodies were found with 3 bullet wounds each a day later. John called another emergency meeting. After addressing the situation, Alex went to the lounge.

Just then, another enormous explosion shook the ship! The lights flickered and went out. Alex ran out of the lounge. There were bits of fire everywhere. Emma was running toward him. Emma shouted over the fire, "**WHAT IS HAPPENING?**" Alex responded with, "**I THINK THIS IS THE END!**" An evil cackle arose. "**I knew you would catch on eventually!**" Alex turned and saw the killer. The killer started laughing maniacally! Another explosion ceased his existence. At the same time, the ship began to tear apart. Alex and Emma looked at each other. Alex wrapped his arms around Emma and hugged her, knowing that this would be the last time he would be in this universe. Before the ship burned up, killing everyone inside, a voice shouted, "**YOU WILL NOT WIN!!!**"

Story IX

Vanished

In this story, Abbadon Evanuit, or Abba Evan for short, is a miner in his 30s, who lives in the town of Coppull in Lancashire, UK. He was born on October 13, 1876. The mining company he works for at a mine named Coppull Collieries. Things suddenly take a turn for the better when he starts mining and finds something that will change his life forever!

Abba could hear the screeching of the train wheels from miles away. He could smell the coal and hear the hiss of the steam and the scream of the horn. It was a gloomy Tuesday evening. Abba was tired and dearly wanted to go home. He checked his pocket watch. It was 8:30 PM. He also checked his detailed calendar. The date was April 9, 1912. The monotone sounds of pickaxes grinding against coal and copper tormented the minds of anyone in the area. Abba wished he could get a 15-pound bonus.[14] The Titanic was setting sail tomorrow at noon, and he wanted to go to the United States for a better job.

---

[14] 15 pounds or 18 dollars would translate to $550 today.

As Abba was mining, he uncovered a bit of silver. As Abba inspected it closer, he noticed there was more to the vein! Abba continued to mine the silver and discovered a small vein of diamonds! Abba ran to the mine owner, who was in his office. When Abba opened the door, he said, "Look! Dr. Clive! I found you some diamonds!" Dr. Clive lowered his half–moon spectacles and stared at the diamonds. He then commented on Abba's work. "Yes…YES! This is exactly what we want! I think this is worth…15 pounds!" Abba was astonished at the probability of wishing for 15 pounds and suddenly getting it! Clive reached his hand in a drawer, pulled out 15 pounds, and handed it over to Abba.

Clive said, "I heard that you were planning on moving to The United States. Is this goodbye?" Abba looked at Clive for a moment. He then realized what Dr. Clive was saying and what he had signed up for. "Yes, tis so." Clive sighed and pulled out a paper of resignation that Abba signed. Clive bid Abba goodnight, and Abba left the mine for good. It was almost a relief for Abba to leave. Abba had worked at the mine for over two decades!

Abba summoned a carriage and rode for 30 minutes back to his house, where he sold his house. It was actually government owned, and the government had all the rights to the house. The only reason he was not evicted was that he worked for the mine. Once Abba had packed everything up, he walked to the train station, and at 2:00 AM, a US Mallard train stopped. Abba got on the train, and 10 minutes later, it started to move. The Mallard was the fastest steam train ever built. Abba rode for about 6 hours to Southampton, England, which is where the ship would be leaving. Abba picked up an Eclair and went to get his ticket for the Titanic. He then saw the glorious ship; the Titanic was enormous! Abba was amazed. A few hours later, the Titanic set sail, and they were off on a journey that would change their lives forever. It was a truly marvelous ship. So many tales about it…some were dark, and many were true!

Once the Titanic started moving, it nearly hit some boats docked nearby! Luckily, no harm was done. Abba made his way to his room. He had gotten a second-class room. Abba was impressed with the beauty of the room. There was a fancy bedside table, a four-poster bed, a shower and toilet, an enormous set of drawers, and a wardrobe! Abba hung up his clothes and sorted all of his luggage out. A stewardess on the Titanic announced that lunch was being served. Abba brought a journal to write about his tales on the boat. One thing that he mentioned in his journal was that the curried chicken was exquisite! Nothing much happened that night. After dinner, Abba played cards with a stranger on board and went to bed. The next morning, Abba went to the library of the Titanic and read A Christmas

Carol. Abba enjoyed reading. After eating some more delectable foods, Abba went to bed.

It went on like this until April 15, 1912. Abba was awoken by the sunlight through the curtains and went to breakfast. He had turkey and biscuits for breakfast. He also played chess with ten other passengers and won every time! For lunch, he had mutton chops. It was quiet on board until dinner when he had the delectable Christmas pudding. After dinner, Abba explored the ship and went to the cargo hold. Abba was fumbling with his ring when it slipped off and fell to the floor. **KABANG!** When the ring hit the floor, an ear-splitting sound reached Abba's ears! It was gone as soon as it had come. Where had the sound come from, Abba wondered? He was confused and concerned.

He sprinted toward the stairs and found his ring next to the bottom stair. It was suddenly slightly corroded! Abba put the ring back on with surprising difficulty and headed back upstairs to his room to see what the commotion was all about. **GONG!** The sound of a clock striking midnight could be heard faintly. People were out and about. Some stewards were calming the people saying, "Nothing is wrong! You can go back to bed!" People eventually went back to their cabins and went back to sleep. Abba decided that the loud sound he had heard was something of concern. Sure, people said the Titanic was unsinkable…but was it really?

When Abba returned to his room, he was settling in for the evening, and he suddenly noticed something. The Titanic was tilting! Not by a lot, but by enough to be a concern, maybe 5 or 10 degrees. Abba grabbed his suitcase, where all of his valuables were stored. The clothes and other items would only cost about two or three pounds if lost.[15] Abba sprinted outside and saw an immense change in the activity flow! There was a crowd of people out of their rooms. Abba was now very worried for the ship! He noticed that a few crew members were handing out life jackets. They were shouting, "The life jackets are just a precaution!" Abba knew that the life jackets were not just a precaution.

He grabbed a life jacket and headed out to the ship's deck. Abba checked the time. It was 12:30 AM. By the look of things, people had finally grasped the dangerous nature of the situation that they were in. Abba walked over to the lifeboats and would have gotten on one if the lifeboat manager had not stopped him and said, "Women and children first!" After spending a while on the ship's deck, Abba looked around and spotted a lifeboat being lowered and quickly jumped into the boat. The boat barely moved yet the people in the lifeboat acted like he nearly capsized the boat! Not to mention, the boat was not even halfway down the ship. The Titanic's lights flickered and died as the boat continued down to the

---

[15] About 100 pounds or 90 dollars today

icy cold ocean below. According to Abba's pocket watch, it was 2:10 AM. The lifeboat hit the water, and they rowed about 50 meters away from the Titanic.

A few minutes later, the ship broke in two! Then the screams started! They were horrible screams for loved ones and friends. Abba was glad that he was in the lifeboat. It was immensely cold. The bow of the Titanic started to sink a few minutes later, and the screams grew ear-piercing! Moments later was the death of all hope for the Titanic. The ship had completely sunk below the surface. The lifeboat he was in rescued three people who had jumped from the Titanic as it sank.

One of the men that Abba rescued was very cold. After pulling him onboard, he suddenly became colder and stopped breathing thirty minutes later. By that point, the screams had been silenced. There was nothing. Nothing but the blankless expanse of ocean and icebergs that had doomed the Titanic. It was agonizingly cold for nearly two hours. Finally, hope arrived! A ship was spotted in the distance. That ship was the Carpathia. The Carpathia arrived at 4:00 AM and loaded the first lifeboat ten minutes later. After an hour or so, Abba was in a hospital bed, asleep. He was exhausted from sleep deprivation and muscle fatigue. Once Abba awoke, he asked one of the Carpathia hospital workers, "How many people died?" She solemnly responded, "We don't know for sure, but we have picked up around 700 passengers from the water." Abba's stomach lurched! That meant over 1,500 people had perished with the ship! He did not expect so many! Abba fell back asleep. On April 18, the Carpathia arrived in New York. As Abba left the Titanic, he had a chocolate bar from the ship. It was his only souvenir. All around him were families mourning the death of their loved ones. Abba had none. He was alone. Abba knew that there would be books and newspapers describing the Titanic disaster in great detail. One day. One day soon…too soon.

OVER 16 MONTHS LATER…
OCTOBER 13, 1913

It had been over a year since the Titanic crashed into the iceberg and sank. He was interviewed about the Titanic incident almost every day for eight months until the talk slowly spread to other topics. Abba was not as traumatized by the Titanic disaster as other people were. However, it still brought tears to his eyes on occasion. Abba now lived in North Carolina and worked at the Cape Hatteras lighthouse. Abba wanted a calm sea life at the lighthouse, but details of the Titanic kept him up at night.

For instance, he had learned that the Titanic was not the Titanic! There were three ships that the White Star Line had built alongside the Titanic. The Olympic had a fire in the mailroom that weakened the boat, and so did the Titanic! When looking at the pictures of the

Titanic, Abba noticed that none of them had burn marks, but Abba recalled that the Titanic did have a burn mark when he had looked at it! So, Abba had a hypothesis that the White Star Line had switched the ships out. Abba knew it was not the Britannic, the third ship, because the Britannic did not look similar to the Titanic or Olympic, while the Titanic and Olympic were nearly identical.

A well-known fact about the Titanic is that there were not enough lifeboats aboard. They needed nearly fifty more lifeboats. And the final truth that Abba learned was that someone had predicted the sinking of the Titanic over a decade before it happened in 1912. The novella is about a fictional British ocean liner named Titan which struck an iceberg and sank! Abba was writing all of these thoughts in his journal and hoped to publish it in a few years. For now, Abba decided it was time to visit a place he had heard and read about…the Bermuda Triangle. It was a place of mystery and paranoia. Abba prepared everything to leave but didn't tell many people because he knew he would be back soon. However, he was never heard from again. Once the local townspeople noticed that Cape Hatteras' light was not lit, they asked the law enforcement to take a look. The law enforcement were confused and did not know what to do. Someone said, "It's like Mr. Evan disappeared! Vanished!"
This was Abba's last journal entry:

October 13, 1913

"It has been over a year since the Titanic sank. I have several speculations regarding the Titanic. Please read the previous journal entries to understand. I am traveling to the Bermuda Triangle, and I may not return. I might vanish."

Story X

Killers Are Watching

This story is a realistic fiction story that takes place in modern times. "Killers Are Watching" is about several serial killers who murder people without a trace! The main character is Michael Vice, and he is 15 years old and lives in Henderson, NC.

Michael awoke to a beautiful rising sun and a windy fall day. It was Sunday. Michael's family went to church on Sunday mornings. Michael put on a red flannel shirt and jeans and had breakfast. He was riding in the car when the radio announced a chilling message. "There is a killer on the loose in Henderson, NC! Please take the necessary precautions for safety. The police are investigating the situation. **Stay alert to stay alive!**" After the radio announcement was finished, the radio turned back to music. Michael was slightly concerned, and for good reason! Multiple people were talking about this killer during Sunday school at the church. Michael thought it was odd that not a single person was talking about who was murdered. After church, he headed to the train tracks hoping to record a video for his YouTube channel, but no trains came by today.

After he was home, nothing much happened, and he went to bed.

The next day, Michael got up for school. He was in the 10th grade. All that the school could talk about over the next week was the murderer. The school was taught more about lockdown drills in case the murderer came onto school premises. That afternoon, Michael was in the school bathroom when he suddenly noticed his reflection was absent! He tried to take the mirror off, but it would not budge. At that very moment, the fire alarm went off. The noise startled Michael so much that he nearly screamed! Michael ran to the hallway and found it completely deserted. There was no longer an alarm going off, and no students were running about the halls trying to get to safety. It was eerily quiet. Michael walked down the hallway back to his math class. At that moment, the *actual* fire alarm went off! This time, Michael did cry out in fear. What did all of this mean? Was he mentally well? Was he still sane? What was the sound in the bathroom that sounded like the fire alarm? Was he a danger to society? All of these thoughts penetrated every corner of his mind.

Michael tried to push the thoughts out of his mind, which worked…at least for now. Michael evacuated the school with all the other students. The school was definitely on fire. The fire department was on the scene five minutes later. It turns out that it was a microwave that had caught on fire. The strangest part was that neither the school nor the fire department knew what was in the microwave that had caused the fire. All signs pointed to the microwave exploding on its own accord. However, who had ever heard of a microwave exploding so spontaneously? Thankfully, no one was injured. School was dismissed for the day, and everyone went home. Michael decided to keep the mirror and fire alarm dilemma a secret for now. He also decided to buy a steel metal plate for a "Tuesday doomsday" scenario, just in case a school shooting were to occur. There was a killer on the loose, so he was trying to be safe! This metal plate would protect Michael and possibly his friends as long as the shooter didn't have armor-piercing bullets.

The next few school days were largely uneventful. The topic of the killer on the loose nearly disappeared until something tragic happened. The bodies of five people were found just one street over from where Michael lived! The police were busy investigating that on Friday of that week, the school's internet was hacked. It was an unsolved mystery! The Federal Bureau of Investigation got involved and was able to restore everything, but they found a data set that was not there before. It was in binary code, and it took the FBI an entire night to decode. It was a threat made to the school and, worse, its students! The school staff and students were worried, and the police were doing their best to offer protection.

The following Wednesday, Michael decided to take a walk and heard something that sent shivers up his spine! Gunshots! There was a rapid series of gunfire nearby, so he ran to investigate. There lay the dead body of one of his friends! Even though he was dead, his body was mutilated in such a way that gunshot wounds couldn't do. It was horrible! He called 911. When the police arrived, they could not see the body; it was as if the body wasn't even there! When Michael went to touch the body, his hand went through him and touched the pavement below. He had hallucinated the whole thing!

Luckily a police officer decided that Michael needed some mental help. They reached out to some psychiatrists and therapists, but unfortunately, that did little to stop the monster from taking over Michael's reality. Once school started back, Michael was cared for, but he still struggled for the next week. Then, the unexpected happened! A lockdown drill! Michael and the entire class were packed into a tiny closet. When the alarm went off, they had been in social studies class, where they were studying the nuclear bomb drills people did in school back in the 1940s and 1950s during the Cold War. So much irony there!

Suddenly, Michael heard footsteps outside the classroom. They had locked the door, but someone opened the door easily! The footsteps echoed loudly against the floor. The intruder stopped in the doorway.

Michael's breath came in hot, sharp pants. He started hyperventilating when the intruder laughed. A cold, heartless laugh sent shivers down Michael's spine. Just then, Michael passed out. When he regained consciousness, he discovered the fact that there was no intruder. The only intruder that had entered the building was the intruder of reality itself in Michael's mind! Michael decided to go to a mental health facility. It helped a little, but not enough.

Michael turned on the news one night only to be greeted with the talk of a new murderer in town. No one knew much about him, but he killed six people. Michael was now worried for the city. On Thursday, he decided to take a walk around town. While he was walking, a laugh rose from behind him! It was the same laugh as the non-existent intruder's laugh! Michael turned around, and screamed, "**don't test my reality!**" The dark shadow of the person laughed and said, "If this reality doesn't exist, then this shouldn't hurt!" With that, the person pulled a gun from a holster and pulled the trigger on Michael. **BANG!**

When police arrived at the scene, they found no gunshot wounds. Instead, Michael's body showed no external signs of death. Michael's death resulted from a severe case of bipolar disorder. Bipolar serious mental health illness that causes most mental health deaths. Michael had no reality.

Story XI

Disappearances

This story is part realistic fiction, part science fiction, and part horror fiction. It takes place inside an abandoned hospital. It starts as a typical game, but things quickly take a turn for the worse when people start disappearing! The main character is me, Caleb Bundon, and the story takes place one year in the future.

Ding! The text from my phone surprised me. I was playing a Roblox game and was not expecting a message. It was a text from one of my friends. "Hey, we found a good place to play Blackout! Big game tomorrow at the abandoned hospital in the link below. A group of 13 from the church are going, including you!" The link led to a hospital in Gastonia on Google Maps. I asked my parents if I could go, and they said yes. So, the next day, I packed a few things for the game and set out for the hospital. I grinned. This was going to be a fun game! It was an exquisite end to the long week of publishing my book. This very book you are in fact reading!

The game Blackout is a game very similar to Among Us. There are a certain number of players and two killers. The killer's job is to double-tap the shoulders of "citizens," and they will drop dead 15 seconds later. They win by killing everyone. The citizens' job is to vote off the killers before they kill the entire crew. They do this at town meetings when a dead body is found, and someone shouts **TOWN MEETING!!!** No flashlights allowed, only whispering. The roles are chosen by selecting cards. In our game, there would be 1 judge, 10 citizens, and 2 killers. The judge is the only position automatically announced. There is one final rule to the game…**DON'T DIE!**

My parents dropped me off at the hospital, and we said our goodbyes and they drove away. Everyone was gathering outside the hospital. The police were notified and agreed that we could use the property for the night if we paid a rental sum to their department. John, one of the group leaders, called us together, and said, "Is everyone here?" He started calling names, and everyone was present. We walked inside the hospital, and Jason, the main leader, closed the door. It was nearly pitch black. After that, John and Jason gave out the cards. John announced, "Please do not show your card to anyone!" Once all the cards were handed out, we looked at our cards. I was a citizen. John was the Judge. Jason said, "Let the game of Blackout…begin!"

With that, everyone dispersed. I started by exploring the hospital. A path was blocked by equipment, and I moved it aside. There was a stairwell nearby, so I took a chance and went up the stairs. Joseph, my best friend, followed me up the stairs. After ensuring he was not a killer, we continued and came across some old dusty beds that made me have a sneezing fit! John came up the stairs and whispered to Joseph and me, "Do you have any suspicions about who the killer is?" I almost backed away as John asked the question, but then realized that John was the Judge and couldn't be a killer. I replied, "Not yet. I have only seen you and Joseph." John nodded and walked away.

We walked up another flight of stairs, and I felt dizzy as the stairs nearly broke under my weight because of the age of the wood. What I saw upstairs was strange. It was a library of sorts. Maybe it was a library of possible secrets! I walked to one side of the bookshelf. There was a letter 'A' on the side of the wood. I continued down the row and found several interesting books. One was titled "How to Aid in Getting Rid of Allergies." I opened it, and at that moment, something happened that nearly made my heart stop! There was a scream, a loud, terrified scream! It stopped as soon as it had come.

I turned to the source of the noise. It had come from upstairs, but the door was blocked. I prayed that whatever happened to the person who screamed was not terrible and that they were safe! I reached for an object in the dark and found a rusted axe next to an empty fire extinguisher box. I ran over to the door where several people were already gathered. I started to break open the boarded-up door, which was very easy due to weathering and exposure to the elements. A few seconds later, we had the door open, and everyone clambered upstairs. What we saw up there we will never forget. It was a body. The body of one of my friends! She was dead in a pool of blood! Spelled out on the floor in blood was the word, "**KILLER!**" It sent shivers not only down my spine but all through my body!

We solemnly carried the body downstairs to the first floor. Everyone was white as chalk! None of them expected this! Jason said, "I don't think anyone did this. I know all of you, and you would not do this! I…that's all I have to say." John then said, "We need to get out of here!" I went over to the door, but as expected, it did not open. I even brought the axe and tried to destroy the door but to no avail! John said, "Joseph, you were talking about that show with games where people faced real consequences in real life. This is similar to that!" Joseph nodded and quietly said, "Unfortunately." John said, "I think we will need to continue playing." Everyone at the table nodded and dispersed once again.

After this, I started my journey back to the library. It was completely deserted. I began to search for mysterious books. One was titled "A Guide to Mental Health." Another was titled "Schizophrenia: What Is It?" It was not until a few minutes later that I found the most interesting book. I was looking in the 'Y' section when I happened to glance at a book titled "Your Future." It was odd. What type of author would write such a title, and why is it in a hospital? I attempted to take the book off the shelf, but it was bound by a chain with a padlock. According to the back of the padlock, it was from the 1910s.

I started to search for a key that would fit the padlock. In the library, there was a front desk for checking books in and out. On the desk were several items coated in a thick layer of dust and spider silk. There was a fountain pen, a library stamp, and a pair of cracked half-moon spectacles. I sat down in the chair and opened a drawer. I expected to find several dead spiders and lots of dust, but there were some other items that I did not expect. A working fountain pen, a bible, and even some quarters, dimes, and pennies. There was also an old-looking book that was very weathered. I couldn't make out anything except the title "Vetus Radix - 1902." No wonder it was so hard to read. It was over 100 years old! I decided to test the lamp on the desk in case the power had not been completely severed from the entire hospital, but I had no luck with the light. I shrugged it off and opened the book "Your Future."

The moment I opened the book, I knew something was amiss. This is what was on the first page. "Dear reader, I hope you are indifferent about your future, for you may meet a gruesome end! You have been warned!" I turned the page. The story started with an interesting person as the main character, who was named Cordis. He, just like me, had published a book and decided to play a game with his friends. Here's where things get interesting. The game was the same game we were playing! The game of Blackout! To add to the mystery, the author mentioned that it occurred at the same hospital we were in! He mentioned that he had heard a scream that night, and when he ran to the door, the door was blocked by metal. He also said a dead body was swimming in a pool of blood! The author also mentioned his discovery of the book I am reading along with this library. I was so confused! How did he discover this book and play this very game that we are playing along with playing it in the very same hospital?!! I kept on reading.

He said this is where he learned that the hospital had played a vital role in the great world wars! He also mentioned that the book went back to when it was created in the early 1800s. I kept reading. Cordis also said that as he read the book, he heard a sound that sent shivers down his spine. Cordis heard a second scream that night and then silence. At that very moment, I was snapped out of my reading by a sound. It was the sound of a gut-wrenching scream! A horrible scream that stopped a few seconds later. My heart stopped for a second. I thought, "This book described a scream. When he finished his little montage, what could happen but a scream!?!?"

I ran to the floor above me. This time, there was no dead body but a trail of blood and footprints leading away from the scene. Then I heard footsteps, so I ran towards them. As I ran, I heard a thud. I ran around the corner and stopped suddenly. It was the dead body of another person! The girl was also one of my good friends. I nearly lost control...how could this be happening? We called the group together and carried the body back to where we had the last meeting. I described what had happened, but I only described the book to John. He believed that it was just a coincidence. I mean, for all I know, it could be! I also mentioned that I had heard someone running away from the body. No one knew what to do.

John said, "I guess we keep playing." After that, I decided to be ten times more careful around everyone. There were 11 players left. I walked up to the library and grabbed the book "Your Future." I then walked past where the previous dead body had been and explored the final floors. The floors were pretty uneventful. I did find some non-perishable food, a microwave, and the roof entrance, but that was it. I sat down on the helipad on the roof and opened the book. I sat there reading the book, completely enthralled by it, not noticing someone creeping up the stairs. I only came out of my trance after hearing two people's screams, but by then, it was already too late!

I ran to the stairs and saw who it was. It was one of my friends! He was one of the killers! He smiled a menacing grin, and at that moment, I realized that the person I once considered a friend was lost. He was not himself. I jumped up and kicked him in the chest. His body hit the cold hard stone and he was knocked out. I shouted, "**TOWN MEETING!**" Everyone arrived on the scene incredibly upset! The two people who had died were very nice individuals and loved by all. Nonetheless, the total number of people alive was now down to nine. I sat down and explained to everyone what had happened. The killer was awake, but no one saw the knife! Some accused me of being the killer. Then, John gave the final words. "We need to vote. All in favor of voting Caleb as the killer, raise your hand." Three people raised their hands, and I don't blame them! I certainly looked guilty!

John then turned to the nervous killer. "All in favor?" Six people raised their hands. The killer had been decided and voted on! John then asked him this. "Are you the killer?" He confirmed being the killer by saying, "Yes." The confirmed killer fell to the ground, and there was a sound as loud as a gunshot when he hit the floor. We gathered around him and checked his pulse. He was dead. Dead and very cold. Cold as ice. No one knew what had happened, and none of us could do anything. We then separated. I went back to the book I had left behind. I flipped the page and let out a gasp! The book stated, "I was very interested in this book, but that was a mistake. The killer snuck up on two people and killed them both. They were on the stairs. I caught the killer red-handed. He died when he was voted off by six of the remaining people. The total now sits at eight. I then proceed back to reading this book."

What was happening?!?! The book was in tune with this reality! My reality! It was mirroring what was happening in real time. I flipped 5 pages forward. They were all blank! My friend Riley then pulled me out of my thought bubble. We were both so disturbed. We agreed we were all put in this situation for a reason. God has a purpose for us here. Whether that is death or life, we don't know. We talked briefly and I showed her the "Your Future" book. I looked down at the book and opened it to where I had left off reading. The blank page after the one I was reading was now filled with words of a similar conversation that the person in this book had with his friend!

Riley noticed my reaction, so I told her everything about the book. She was shocked! Once I had told her everything, we went our separate ways. So did the characters in the story "Your Future." I thought to myself, "This just keeps getting weirder and weirder all the time!" I was walking down to the kitchen when suddenly, **CRACK!** I fell through the floor! Well, at least I got to the kitchen quickly! Joseph was there too. We looked at each other, and both laughed. I opened one of the cabinets and found an iron flask labeled "Almond Water." When I opened it, I was greeted with the aroma of several smells, including almond, vanilla, rose water, and a faint butter scent. When I tasted it, it was sweet. I said, "Weird!" Joseph looked up. I searched and found another bottle of "Almond Water" and gave it to Joseph. We talked for a little bit before going our separate ways.

I opened the book. It described the author giving his best friend "Cashew Water." How bizarre! I walked to the hospital ward and continued reading. I heard a loud thump. Could it be another body? I jumped up, grabbed a scalpel off the table, and ran to the door. There lay the body of Joseph. Dead. I screamed with the strength of ten-thousand voices! "**TOWN MEETING!!**" I was devastated by the death of Joseph. No one expected it. No one wanted it to happen. No one knew anything. No one knew my pain. **No one.**

We could not vote on anyone, so we skipped it and continued. It took a lot to hold back the tears. I won't lie that some escaped! I was reading my book when

Riley came up to me. We were both saddened. We talked for a little bit before Riley left. At that moment, I heard a sound that I did not want to hear. I heard a slicing sound, a grunt, and the thud of another body falling. I screamed! Tears streamed from my eyes as I ran toward the murderer. I felt a searing pain in my chest...I looked down only to be greeted by blood. I had been stabbed! My vision went blurry, and I fell to the ground. Everything went black. I was dead. But how am I still writing this if I am dead? We did not just die...We disappeared into the void of the stars.

Story XII

The Never-Ending Hotel

This story is based on two main things. The Roblox horror game called Doors, and the famous Disney World ride named The Twilight Zone Tower of Terror. I won't tell you what they are about because the fear of the unknown is best if you know nothing about it! This story took place on October 30, 1939. The main character is Salem Mails. He is in his thirties and has a job as a train conductor. He hears about a popular hotel in Hollywood, California, and decides to visit there. Videos are on my YouTube page!

"The air is not so pure today," several workers grumbled to Salem. He smiled. He had been working here for nearly ten years and knew the air in this area was cleaner than any factory air! It was Friday night, and the workers were going home soon. A few minutes later, they were dismissed. After being dismissed, Salem walked over to the taxi, hopped in, and asked the taxi driver to drive him to his house. Once he was there, he had dinner and went to bed. The following day, he woke up to the hustle and bustle of the city traffic. Salem made a cup of hot cocoa and was sitting in an armchair by the fireplace when there was the sound of a knock on the door. He walked over to the door and opened it to be greeted with a newspaper. Salem opened the newspaper and read the front page:

The Portae Hotel Opened to Wonderful Reviews!

The Portae hotel opened less than a month ago and has been a huge success! Now that Halloween is approaching, a single bedroom is only $12.99![16]

Continue on page 5…

Salem decided to stay at the hotel for a weekend. He booked the 2-hour train from Barstow to Hollywood. After he arrived, he checked into the hotel and took the elevator to his floor. The rattling of the elevator was immense. The elevator doors slid open to reveal a deserted atrium. Salem thought it was odd that he had just taken the elevator out of the atrium, but this atrium was different. No hallways had rooms to sleep in. Salem stepped out of the elevator, and the doors closed behind him. There was a fire in a fireplace to his left, and to his right was a desk with a service bell, luggage, a luggage cart, and a rack for keys. There was a key on the rack. Straight ahead was a door with the number 1 carved into it. Salem went over to the door and noticed

---

[16] About $275 today.

it had a large padlock on it. Salem predicted that the key on the rack fitted the door. He reached under the luggage cart and grabbed the key. Sure enough, the key opened the door.

However, instead of being greeted with a hallway with different bedrooms, it was deserted! Apart from a set of drawers, 3 bookshelves, shrubs to Salem's left and right, and another door, it was empty! He decided to ask the man at the front desk downstairs, so he returned to the elevator. When he pushed the down arrow, there was no response from the elevator! He pressed all the buttons to no avail. Salem decided there was probably another elevator on the other side of the door, so he continued through the doorway. He was then greeted with several more bookshelves and a wardrobe. How odd that there was a wardrobe in the middle of the hallway! Salem opened it, but it was empty. He closed it and walked around the small area.

There was another door at the back of the hallway with a padlock and a number 3 on it. On the opposite end was a door that did not have a number. Salem was curious and opened the door. It was a room with a desk, 3 bookshelves, a wardrobe, 2 armchairs, and a bed. On the right armchair was the key for door 3. The bed was tempting, but Salem thought, "It can't hurt to explore a little further!" Salem snatched the key off of the armchair and opened the door. Yet another room met him. This time, a few stairs led to a lower level with a boarded-up door. Salem continued through this door and found more of the same. The same gloomy room with the same objects. He hardly troubled himself over it. He proceeded through another door at the back of this room. There was a gloomy-looking window to the left.

He looked outside at the endless pouring of rain. There was nothing else to be seen out of the window. After going through another door, Salem was again met with another hallway. When he turned to his left, he was met with 2 sets of drawers. One chest of drawers had 3 pencils, coins, a letter, and an ink container. The next set of drawers had more coins, which was the only helpful thing found in the drawers so far. And again, he found another door at the back of this hallway, so he ventured through the doorway.

This time, he was met with a different sight! There was a locked steel door and stairs leading to a basement. Salem walked down the stairs and found an assortment of barrels next to the wall. When he walked around for a moment, he flipped a switch that he found on the wall and went back toward the stairs. The steel door had swung open to another door that Salem went through. He was finally met with a hallway with rooms on both sides. This was the strangest hotel he had ever visited! He went to the first door on the right to see a bedroom. The door opened easily. He heard a falling noise from nearby, so he quickly darted out of the room and into another room to investigate. He didn't think the sound had come from this room, but how strange! That was the first sound he had heard since taking the elevator ride up to the hallways!

He began searching for the second room he was in. It contained a set of drawers with more coins in it. He then left the room and went to another room where the falling/knocking might have come from. In this room, more coins were found. Salem continued searching until he found the key to the next door. While searching, he heard a noise that sounded like it was coming from under the bed. As he moved closer, a mysterious force pushed him away from the bed! It had no visible body! After going through the next door, he was greeted with the same uninteresting sight and yet another key and door. Once he went through the next door, Salem's perspective changed! Straight ahead was a fireplace, and to the sides were paintings with shapes behind the paintings.

Salem walked further into the room and saw a desk. On that desk was an item that Salem had not seen before...a lighter! Not the modern-day lighters but the ones that were popular in the 1900s. The paintings looked mismatched and were all different shapes and sizes. Salem took one painting off the wall to investigate the shapes. There was a square behind it. It then clicked with Salem! He was supposed to rearrange the paintings to fit the shapes behind them! It took him a little while, but Salem managed to get all the paintings in the right place. Once he moved the last painting to the correct location on the wall, the fireplace sunk beneath the floor and revealed yet another door!

Salem walked through the door, and the lights began to flicker. Salem decided to explore one of the wardrobes in the room, and it was lucky that he did! There was a loud and very terrifying screaming sound, followed by a roaring sound similar to a freight train rolling by, combined with lights breaking! It was gone just as quickly as it had come. Salem quickly walked out of the wardrobe and through the next door. When he opened this door, the lights were off! Salem lit his lighter and leaned against a wall.

He was still leaning against the wall when a hissing sound met his ears. Salem was confused because the sound had not come from the lighter. Just then, a weird entity that was the color of oil came out of the nothingness and bit his chest! The pain sent him to the floor, but even though he was in much pain, he was able to get up. He turned around and looked the thing in the eye. It screeched and disappeared! Salem thought this was incredibly odd and knew he had to get out of there as soon as possible! Suddenly he heard another hiss, and the entity bit him once more. He was dead before he hit the floor.

Story XIII

The Backrooms

The Backrooms is an urban legend or creepy pasta about a seemingly infinite expanse of randomly generated office complexes and other environments. It is known to have the smell of moist carpets, walls of dull yellow paint, and the infinite and unending sound of fluorescent lights. There are different levels of the Backrooms, but all have one thing in common. They're dangerous! To get to the Backrooms, you must "no-clip" out of reality into a matrix. An infinite-and-nearly-unending matrix. There are a few things found in the Backrooms that try to help you, which the main character will encounter. Our main character is 24 years old, and his name is Fred Walker. The date is May 12, 1998.[17]

The monotonous sound of typing on the keyboards and dial-up internet transfers were very discomforting to Fred's ears. All he wanted to do was go home. He was new to his job, and it was difficult organizing all of

---

[17] For more information, visit:
https://en.wikipedia.org/wiki/The_Backrooms

the numbers and shipping routes. A few minutes later, everyone started packing up and heading home. Fred turned off the computer he was working on and packed it up. It had been a long day, and he just wanted to lay in his bed and go to sleep. Walking home in the rain, he thought, "My life is on autopilot. What can I do to make my life interesting and not make every day the same thing?! I can't quit my job for several years."

As he was thinking this, a car swerved, and in the blink of an eye, he was soaked. Fred kept walking until he was home. He removed his rain jacket and wet clothes and jumped onto his bed. He drifted off to sleep, and in his dreams, he wished to be anywhere but in this world. He hoped for something to make his life interesting.

When he woke up, he was in a different place. A place of dull yellow. A place that smelled of moist socks coming from the carpet. A place where entities ensure no escape with the help of the hundreds upon millions of square miles of randomly generated office complexes. A place where there is almost no chance of survival. Fred got up and looked around. He said aloud, "Where am I? What is this place?" The carpet muffled his voice. Fred walked over to a light. "Strange," he thought. The light was flickering along with the buzz of the fluorescent light.

Fred walked some more, and he heard a thudding sound. It was then that Fred realized he was not alone. There was something else here! Fred looked around. There was nothing in sight. Nothing but the dull-yellow walls and the flickering lights of the Backrooms. Fred did not know what to do! Would he be trapped here for all eternity? Or would he find a way out? Fred remembered what a wise man had once said to him at a concert. "Inveniam viam aut faciam." This roughly translates to "I will either find a way or forge one." Fred repeated this to himself and started walking. The repetitive nature of the Backrooms ensured that Fred expected no end. However, he never gave up.

A day later, he was thirsty and starving. He was praying that he would find anything that would quench his thirst and satisfy his hunger. A few minutes later, he thought he was hallucinating when he saw thermoses by one of the many walls in the Backrooms. As he moved closer, he could see that he was not hallucinating, and he ran to the thermoses! He opened them up and was greeted with an aroma of almonds. Fred thought this was strange, but he drank anyway. The taste was sweet with an almond butter flavor. Fred downed all three thermoses in a matter of a minute! He got up and continued forward. He was very energized by the "Almond Water" drink he had encountered. He was content…for now. It only takes one bad thing to happen to change your mood completely!

Unfortunately, this is exactly what happened to Fred. He was walking around when he heard a light break. He was curious about what caused it to break. So he jogged toward the source of the noise. That was a big mistake! Fred turned the corner and was greeted with something black where the light had once been. It was the darkest substance that you could imagine! It dripped from the ceiling where the light had been and emitted an odd sound. It was the kind of sound you get if you place a microphone too close to a speaker. It was a sinister sound, an evil sound. A sound that threatens to envelop you until you cease to exist! Fred backed away quickly.

The lights flickered again. Fred heard the sound of glass breaking and felt glass hit his shoulder! He backed away hurriedly and just in time! Fred was so terrified he started running! His vision became blurred. More glass was shattering all around him. It was overwhelming! Suddenly, everything stopped. It was strange. Just seconds ago, glass was raining down from the ceiling, and the next second was peaceful. Fred tripped as he ran and saw that there were glass shards everywhere. The black goo was dripping from the lights in a rhythmic-like pattern. It was unsettling and made Fred's stomach crawl. Or was that the hunger that enveloped him?

He may have escaped the chaos of the black goo, but he did not escape the hunger for food and the thirst for water! They still possessed him! Fred started once again searching for food and water. It took him two days to find food and water. For Fred, it felt like two months! He didn't know how long he was in the Backrooms because he had no way of telling the date and time. He entered a sort of room where he found six thermoses and a box labeled "Royal Rations." Inside the box, he found a rectangle of a white substance similar to gelatin and the Bible verse Exodus 3:8. Fred consumed the whole rectangle in seconds and opened the thermoses. This time, only 4 of the drinks tasted like "Almond Water." One had a rotten milk taste, and the other tasted like cashews! Still, he drank all of them.

After that, he continued forward. Another day passed. He noticed that it had gotten steadily colder. Fred was almost overtaken with chills, the same type of chills you get when you have a fever. His throat was sore, and he suddenly had a stuffy nose. Fred also had extreme muscle pain and fatigue. He started to notice it when he could hardly walk. However, he pushed on and found some more "Almond Water." Three more days passed, and Fred could hardly go on. He had consumed no food or water for many days! Surprisingly, Fred stumbled upon two more packs of "Royal Rations" and several containers of "Almond Water" that he drank contently.

While Fred was consuming the precious goods, he heard a noise he was not expecting to hear. He heard more cracking of glass sounding above him, and glass rained down on him. He sprinted out of the way just in time! The black goo was back! Once it had cleared, he looked up. He saw a peculiar creature standing a distance away from him. It did not notice Fred in the slightest. It had a weird android appearance but looked like it was made with thick wires. It was oddly eerie, with an almost menacing demeanor about it. A voice in Fred's head told him to run and not investigate it, but instead, he walked toward it. He was a short distance away when it suddenly turned its head toward Fred. He muttered instinctively, "Hello."

The creature screamed and started running toward Fred. Fred screamed and started sprinting away from the creature. The creature caught up with little effort and grabbed Fred's legs. Fred let out a scream that would haunt anyone who heard it. Bullets rained down from unknown forces, and the creature dropped Fred. Instead of his head hitting the moist, cold ground, it slipped through the pages of reality. Fred opened his eyes to a dark world with little light in it. He was back in the real world. Or…was he? Suddenly, a loud car horn sounded. Fred turned his head and **BANG!** He was hit! He was knocked out.

Fred awoke in a hospital bed connected to an assortment of machinery. A doctor noticed he was awake, so he asked Fred for the details of what he had endured. It turns out that Fred was diagnosed with Influenza, sleep deprivation, insomnia, both cognitive and muscle fatigue, and a major internal hemorrhage, not to mention several broken bones from the car. Luckily, Fred was treated quickly, and the doctors decided to give Fred a few tests. The first showed that Fred was mildly disturbed and preoccupied with health problems, and that he struggled with both sleep deprivation and anxiety. Further research showed that he could have panic attacks and nightmares frequently. The doctors were slightly concerned, so they gave him an IQ test, on which he scored an 80. That was a little lower than the national IQ of 100. As the doctor was leaving, Fred heard the doctor mention the date…it was 2006! They had moved 8 years into the future! Fred told the staff at the hospital what was happening. He also found out that he was in Nebraska.

Suddenly, Fred woke up from the nightmare that enveloped him!

Be wary of where you step, for you might fall through the pages that make up our world!

Afterword

Thank you for reading *Nightmares Around Us*. Life is filled with unexpected turns. Some of them are nightmares. Some will teach you a lesson. Some will not. It is essential to see the light. However, in the stories that you have read, the light does not exist!

Be sure to check out my YouTube channel called DarkIceeGamer.

www.ingramcontent.com/pod-product-compliance
Lightning Source LLC
Chambersburg PA
CBHW071014120626
46546CB00003B/1078